is it just me or is
everything shit?

is it just me or is everything shit?

insanely annoying modern things

by STEVE LOWE and ALAN McARTHUR
with BRENDAN HAY

GRAND CENTRAL
PUBLISHING

NEW YORK BOSTON

Grand Central Publishing
Hachette Book Group
237 Park Avenue
New York, NY 10017

Visit our Web site at www.HachetteBookGroup.com.

Printed in the United States of America

Originally published in two volumes in 2005
and 2006 by Little, Brown Book Group Ltd.

First Grand Central Publishing Edition: November 2008
10 9 8 7 6 5 4 3 2 1

Grand Central Publishing is a division of Hachette Book Group, Inc.
The Grand Central Publishing name and logo is a trademark of
Hachette Book Group, Inc.

Library of Congress Cataloging-in-Publication Data

Lowe, Steve
Is it just me or is everything shit? : insanely annoying modern things / Steve Lowe and Alan McArthur.—1st ed.
p. cm.
ISBN-13: 978-0446-19788-5
1. Life—Humor. 2. English wit and humor. I. McArthur, Alan. II. Title.
PN6231.L48L69 2008
818'.602—dc22

2008004499

Book design by Charles Sutherland

is it just me or is
everything shit?

A

ABSTINENCE PROGRAMS

Prophylactics may sound like the sort of word you'd find in the Bible ("And He did say unto the Prophylactics . . ."), but it isn't. Prophylactics are a modern scourge, a modern scourge that are sadly prone to bursting and making you die. Jesus, just to be absolutely clear about this, did not like them. He didn't put them on his head at parties. And He didn't put them on his willy.

This is, roughly speaking, the main lesson of abstinence programs: godly guidance in how not to do it. What makes this a particularly difficult campaign is that it's aimed at teenagers, who, as we know, often get quite worked up about sex, finding the whole thing something of a turn-on.

The non-doing-it movement has in recent years been backed by George Bush, Pope Benedict, and, of course, a pre-marriage Jessica Simpson. It will solve so many problems: STDs and pregnancy in the West, AIDS in Africa, all sorts. To help it catch on with teens, the movement has even created an accessory: "purity rings." Purity rings aren't some sort of exotic sex toy; they're rings you wear as a pledge not to bang before marriage. "With this ring, I wed Jesus, who doesn't do it," is what the wearers say.

The wearers are dedicatedly not into joining what Silver Ring Thing movement founder Denny Pattyn called "the cess-pool generation." Ooh, smelly. Again, a Silver Ring Thing is not a sex toy. Just so we're clear on that.

But how can anyone think that sex is not going to happen because of Jesus? How is the sex not going to happen? In fact, an eight-year study in the United States showed that 88% of people taking pledges of abstinence fall off the non-screw wagon before marriage, which for young girls leads to one common result: They start to look more like Britney Spears. Nowadays. All puffy, lugging around car seats.

In the spirit of evenhandedness, we have thoughtfully created some advertising slogans for future campaigns against bumping fuzzies, ever:

- PHALLIC SNEEZES SPREAD DISEASES
- DON'T GO AROUND DOING IT!
- DO DO DON'T DONG DONG, DO DO DON'T DONG
- ONLY LET GOD TOUCH YOU, NOT SOME HORMONE-CRAZED SEX FIEND
- GET OFF THAT PENIS!
- JESUS!

ADS FOR CREDIT CARDS

"Taxi to the airport: $48. Ticket to Kansas City: $428. Spending Christmas together: Priceless." No, add up those other expenses and you'll see it actually cost quite a bit.

"My life is far from ordinary. That's why my card is American Express." Yes, only American Express is open-minded enough to handle your decadent, orgy-filled lifestyle. Visa or Discover? A bunch of bigoted prudes.

Your life is not exciting enough, quite simply, because you haven't borrowed enough money. That much should be self-evident. Borrowing money may make you taller. You will have a nicer smile, and have read more books—while still finding time for that all-important Jet-Skiing holiday. It's possible that, by borrowing money, you can end all wars. Certainly if you get one of Bono/American Express's Red Cards (where a tiny percentage of your capricious spending is forwarded on to the poor, starving African babies) and you spend, spend, spend enough with it—you know, really absolutely totally ruining yourself—you could end famine. All of this while living in a cool contemporary apartment drinking crisp white wine.

ADVENTURERS/MOUNTAINEERS/EXPLORERS

Bong! This is the news: Some bloke with more money than sense has got himself lost on a small dinghy in the middle of the Pacific Ocean. Sorry, when we said *"news,"* we actually meant "waste of everyone's time."

The world being largely explored now, is there really any need for a load of posh jackasses to try to reach the South Pole living only on roasted peat and using equipment they bought on sale at Patagonia? (Note to any posh jackasses reading this: That's a rhetorical question—there is no need for a load of posh jackasses to try to reach the South Pole living only on roasted peat and using equipment they bought on sale at Patagonia. We will, however, let you know if this situation changes.) If they do set out over the Pacific in an eight-foot dinghy, risking almost certain drowning, would it be unreasonable to suggest that when they do capsize, rather than expect a multithousand-dollar rescue operation and media furor, they could at least have the decency to drown, quietly?

These richie riches say things like, "If you make a mistake in that situation, you're dead." Well, don't do it then, you schmuck! Because it's at least feasible that you'll make a mistake! Also: "If the weather closes in, you're dead." Well, forgive me, but isn't that what the weather does in the mountains? "At that point, the weather started to close in!" Of course it did. You were climbing up a fucking mountain.

As re-created in the acclaimed documentary *Touching the Void,* mountaineers Joe Simpson and Simon Yates decided to be the first to climb the treacherous west face of the Siula Grande in the Peruvian Andes. What happened? They made a mistake and the weather closed in. Simpson fell badly, breaking his leg and forcing the bone through his kneecap, causing unimaginable agony. Then, after Simpson fell over a precipice, Yates, thinking his partner dead, cut the rope and his friend fell a hundred more feet into a crevasse. Pulling down the rope, Simpson realized he was alone and almost certain to die. At this point he cracked and started punching the ice wall, yelling: *"Stupid stupid stupid cunt! Cuuuunt!!! Stupid cunt! Stupiiiiddd!!! Cuuunnnttt!!"*

A moment of clarity that, all things considered, he might have had in his living room in Britain. The stupid cunt. [See **Waits on Everest.**]

AIRBRUSHING CIGARETTES OUT OF HISTORY

Sorry, but it did happen. I know, it's shocking. But some people smoked. I'm getting all upset just remembering it, to be honest. It was barbaric. Thank the heavens it's not for us twenty-first-century-ites, though. Oh, no. We don't even know what cigarettes are. What are cigarettes?

Given the stresses inherent in our era, it seems we might have picked the wrong century to quit smoking. But as other dangers pile up, it is kind of good to know that we have tidied away one of the dangers: passive smoking. And the related danger of passively looking at pictures of cigarettes.

The Bibliothèque nationale de France airbrushed a cancer stick from a poster of the famously chain-smoking philosopher Jean-Paul Sartre (it might make people feel *nausée*). The U.S. Post Office corrected a stamp of blues legend Robert Johnson to remove the cigarette dangling from his lips. You can go down to the crossroads to do a deal with the devil, just as long as you don't buy any smokes while you're there. Why not also alter his mouth to make the miserable bastard look a bit smilier, too? "Cheer up, Rob." "Can't. Got hellhounds on my trail."

The Beatles have become such a smoke-free zone that you almost suspect that the next time you hear "A Day in the Life," new lyrics will find Paul McCartney going upstairs to have a vegetarian sandwich. In 2006, the *Capitol Albums Vol. 2* box set removed cigarettes from three smoking Beatles. Before, a cigarette was airbrushed from Paul's hand on the *Abbey Road* cover—and the song titles were altered from "You Never Give Me Your Money (to Buy Fags)," "Carry Those Fags," and "Her Majesty (Doesn't Like Fags Much, But Her Sister Likes Them a Lot)."

ALPHA MALES

Does your boss sprawl over his chair like he's got two prickly pineapples for testicles? Does he clearly consider murder when faced with a promotion competitor? Does he strut around believing all female employees are mere seconds from dragging him to the bathroom for a short, sharp nooner? If so, he probably considers himself an "alpha male": the kind of business/politics top dog who treats everyone else as his bitch—like the Marquis de Sade with a flip chart.

It's amazing how many people swallow this stuff—that a man's at his best when he's at his most animal—despite the seemingly obvious fact that we are, in fact, humans. In his doomed U.S. presidential election campaign in 2000, Al Gore was implored by image consultant Naomi Woolf to discover the brooding sex panther within. In 2004, John Kerry had to go out and shoot at ducks. If this process accelerates, we'll soon be choosing our leaders by getting two beefy Nazis to have a penis-bashing contest in a pit. Dominance hierarchies in the animal kingdom were discovered in the 1920s by Norwegian scientist Thorleif Schjelderup-Ebbe. Studying flocks of hens, he noticed how each member recognized its place above and below its peers; the upper echelons got first dibs at the corn (hence the phrase *pecking order*) and peace generally reigned. *Clever hens,* thought Thorleif Schjelderup-Ebbe.

But applying the same concept to *Homo sapiens* isn't that clever—unless we want our leaders to do head jabs at their opponents' faces before squatting down in the corner for a crap (actually, that might be interesting). In fact, most alpha males are a brain-rotting liability. Look at our current alpha-male-in-chief, President George W. Bush, a man so virile he could inseminate a lump of coal. When he grants the poor, unwashed media a rare audience, he seems to believe that his rugged rudeness makes all journalists, female and male, want to adorn his body with oils. One worries that when he leaves office, the press corps will miss his verbal spankings so terribly that they may compensate by beating each other with rocks after work.

But surely Bush's alpha-male qualifications only ever amounted to graceless egomania, the addition of "Heh heh" to the presidential lexicon, and an endless war in Iraq. Before the UK version of the TV show *Big Brother* 6 began, a contestant named Maxwell predicted he would be the house alpha male. By Day 11, he was demonstrating his lead-dog qualities by instigating a competition with housemate Anthony to see who could be first to pee in his pants. Wondering what stunt they could pull next, Anthony suggested: "We could shit ourselves."

That's where trying to be an alpha male gets you. Think on, Mr. President.

ALT-COUNTRY

Isn't hip-hop the real "alternative" to country music? Regardless, here are some important facts about alt-country-singer-songwriter-whiny-bastard Ryan Adams:

1. Add a *B* to the start of his name and you get "Bryan Adams."
2. Ryan Adams really hates this first fact.

At one gig in Nashville, an audience member satirically shouted for Bryan Adams's 1985 hit "Summer of '69." Ryan Adams singled out the offender and refused to play another note until he left the venue. He even offered him $30 of his own money as a refund. It's Bryan Adams I feel sorry for. No one should have to be associated with alt-country.

ANTI-AMERICANISM

You cannot escape the point: America has produced a vibrant culture that is the pleasure and envy of millions. We have given the world not only Larry the Cable Guy but also "Love in an Elevator" by Aerosmith. Take that, Belgium!

But despite all these achievements, a wave of anti-Americanism is sweeping the globe. In Indonesia in April 2006, people rioted against *Playboy*—not because it was porn per se, but because it was American porn. "Down with Yankee tail"—that might have been the slogan. Apparently, even Japanese porn was deemed comparatively harmless—which is weird, considering it basically consists of women dressed up as little girls.

In Europe, Americans have been traditionally ridiculed for being clamorous, rotund morons who have to be forcibly stopped from eating the furniture. This is all good clean family fun. But now it's getting out of hand with supposedly rational souls seeing Islamists holding up posters proclaiming GOD IS GREAT AND AMERICA IS EVIL and thinking: *Hey, I'll have some of that. Surely I can harness that enthusiasm for the forces of good . . . Hey, you know what? America* is a *Great Satan. Eight euros—that's what going to see* Big Momma's House 2 *cost me . . . the bastards!*

If only the rest of the world could understand that people who just happen to have all been born in the same country are, perhaps, not some strange homogeneous Other. Sure, we Americans have never managed to tell any of you people apart, but c'mon! Have we no flesh? (And plenty of it, quite often.) Do we not bleed? It's a simple matter of divorcing the idea of the American state going around doing all the bad things from the people who live under it. They aren't the same thing. And we didn't even all vote for Idiot Boy. That map of the States after the 2004 presidential election—the sea of blue down the coasts, the red down the middle—didn't tell the whole story. In most of the blue states, nearly 50% voted red, and vice versa. We are a diverse people.

So now, more than ever, our foreign brothers and sisters, we ask you to demonstrate solidarity with our fine (if often quite fat) people—perhaps by watching some Adam Sandler films while eating string cheese. We as a human race must remain confident in the potential of the American people. We believe they are deserving and capable of human liberty. If we would just pull our fat fingers out of our fucking asses. We thank you.

ARCTIC MONKEYS

Listen, we here in America are grateful for the first British Invasion. Without it, we'd be a nation of folksingers, which means we'd also be a nation of sensitive ponytail guys. That said, UK, can you quit forcing the Arctic Monkeys on us. We don't care how many *Spin* lists they top; they're bratty, sloppy MySpace poseurs who are so preciously calculated, they make the Strokes look like the Ramones. They receive praise for stuffing their lyrics full of social realism, but they're a bunch of teens from the suburbs. Their social realism is having a fake ID rejected. The only innovative thing the Arctic Monkeys ever did was put their music online . . . the same as every other unsigned band. Oh, but they got rich off it. So they're what, the musical equivalent of LonelyGirl15?

Of course, everyone's middle-of-the-road nowadays. Even New Wave guitar-tykes who sing state-of-the-nation songs about prostitution. From occupying the cutting edge of Western social advancement (in terms of sex, class, race, peace, the big stuff), albeit often not that seriously, many bands now seem to find the cutting edge a bit, well, sharp. And, unfortunately, quite edgy.

Right alongside the Monkeys are the Kaiser Chiefs, who were apparently mildly perturbed to hear that the local police played "I Predict a Riot" before heading out on Friday nights. But this is hardly in the same league as Reagan appropriating Springsteen's "Born in the USA." There wasn't any message there to rewrite. Anyway, it's surely the Kaisers to a T: *American Idol* indie, the perfect soundtrack for people who don't really like music, but do like to beat up on drunks.

Of course, the Kaiser Chiefs are just one of the New Wave of Careerist Bands Whose Careerism Makes Them Nowhere Near Interesting Enough to Sustain a Career. It's often all in the name. Franz Ferdinand—music bloggers' previous "Greatest Band Ever to Live; Listen to Them, Then Clap Your Ears Until You Go Deaf Because There Is Nothing Else You Ever Need to Hear" titleholder—is in reference to neither a dead archduke nor a disco-dancing German man (what, *Franz Ferdinand* doesn't evoke that image in your mind?). The band only chose the name because, according to bassist Bob Hardy, "Mainly we just like the way it sounded. We liked the alliteration." Lead singer Alex Kapranos added, "Basically a name should just sound good . . . like music." Sorry, but no. A name should "just sound good," fair enough, but the music? The music should kick motherfucking ass. Or at least be more interesting than the name.

ARGUMENTS BETWEEN EQUALLY OBJECTIONABLE CELEBRITIES

When Tommy Lee calls Kid Rock a "jealous no career having country bumpkin."

Or when Kid Rock punches out Tommy Lee.

Or when Christina Aguilera attacks Britney Spears, calling her wedding "trashy" and "pathetic."

Or when Britney Spears calls Christina Aguilera "scary."

Or when *The Hills*'s Spencer Pratt describes castmate Lauren Conrad as "the douche, the psycho."

Or when Keith Olbermann declares Bill O'Reilly "today's worst person in the world."

Or when Jacques Chirac says George W. Bush "is so stupid it's amazing he can eat stuff."

Or when Donald Trump labels Mark Cuban a "loser."

Or when Donald Trump brands Richard Branson a "total failure."

Or when Donald Trump declares Rosie O'Donnell a "fat slob."

Or when Rosie O'Donnell writes that Donald Trump is a "slug."

Or when Danny Bonaduce throws Johnny Fairplay over his head, face-first, knocking out a couple of his teeth.

Why don't you all just play nicely?

ARTICLES IN NEWSPAPERS REPORTING POLLS IN MAGAZINES

For example, saying that Duran Duran's 1995 release *Thank You* is the worst album of all time, according to a poll by *Q* magazine. Or that Matt Damon is the sexiest man alive, according to some publishing monkeys. Reading a magazine does not constitute gathering the news. It constitutes reading a magazine.

What next? Maureen Dowd's new column reveals "Woman Finds Happiness with Sister's Widower . . . riveting True Story in *Glamour* . . . Of course they still miss her . . . And the next thing they knew, they were having sex."

B

BABY NAME BOOKS

Nobody has ever found a good name in a baby name book because most of the entries are things like Hadrian, Dylis, Mortimer, and Binky. Oh yes, and Adolf.

The UK's Collins Gem version genuinely points out under the entry for Adolf/Adolph that "Adolph and the latinised form of the name Adolphus have never been common names in this country and received a further setback with the rise of Adolph Hitler."

Setback? I'll say.

BAD BOYS

"We know it's wrong, but they're just so . . . so . . . likely to commit random acts of violence! Yeah?"

Amy Winehouse and Blake Fielder-Civil. Britney Spears and Kevin Federline. Kate Moss and Pete Doherty. Pamela Anderson and every man she's slept with except Scott Baio. It's official: For today's thrill-seeking chick, a bad boy is the ultimate accessory. Essentially, if your man has never been charged with assault while dealing out meth from his Harley, is he even a man at all? *Booooring!*

In *Observer Woman* magazine, British socialite and ex-Mrs. Noel Gallagher, Meg Mathews, revealed: "Bad boys are always the most attractive . . . When I look back at all my exes, they've all of them either been in prison or rough-and-ready or rock-and-roll. The last one was in prison for 10 months. I thought it was great. I thought I was in *Married to the Mob.* I used to go on the visits all dressed up." And if she was really lucky, he'd shiv her initials into his cellmate. Oh well, at least this finally explains the popularity of *Prison Break.*

Next week: "My new man is Radovan Karadzic. He's been on the run from the UN War Crimes Tribunal for murder, plunder, and genocide since 1996! Genocidal Bosnian Serbs? That's hot!"

BAR TOILET ADS FOR BAR TOILET ADS

REACH AN AUDIENCE OF THOUSANDS EVERY DAY!

IT'S CLEAR WHY 12,000 PANELS LIKE THIS ONE CAN REACH AN AUDIENCE OF 15 MILLION.

It makes a nice change from photos of women going insane thanks to Axe Body Spray, or begging pleas to please watch Spike TV. But it's not a good ad for ads, as they have no ads, just ads for ads telling you how effective their ads would be, if they had any. Which they don't. And that's not a good ad for their ads . . . them not actually having any. Adman, you're a bad adman, man.

BLACKBERRIES

What exactly the fuck do you think you're doing to yourselves?

BLING

Louis XIV was big pimping. Imelda Marcos is a powerballin' bee-yatch. Zsa Zsa Gabor? The motherfucking bomb.

By the late 1990s, hip-hoppers had abandoned all pretence of fighting the powers that be. Instead, most had become the kinds of cartoon money-grabbing capitalists that could slip neatly into a Soviet propaganda film—except replacing the bushy mustaches and top hats with hos. Once it took a nation of millions to hold them back. Now it takes a nation of millions to hold their coats.

The word was *bling*—a coinage from New Orleans rapper B. G. of the wonderfully named Cash Money Millionaires collective (hmm, definitely a money theme developing here) to describe light glistening in diamonds. His 1999 U.S. smash "Bling Bling" portrayed a fantastic world of Mercs, platinum rings, diamond-encrusted medallions, helicopters, and drinking so much fine booze that you end up vomiting everywhere (bet you didn't know that was cool, did you?).

In a startlingly widespread display of Stockholm syndrome, the ideal for urban kids suddenly involved transforming yourself from ordinary human into monomaniac money machine. By 2004, the Roc's PR Strategy, a business plan for Jay-Z/Damon Dash's* Roc-A-Fella music/clothing/ booze/jewelry corporation,

---

* Dash famously refuses to wear any item of clothing twice, but does it count if he goes swimming? When he gets out of the bath—and presuming he hasn't lost his locker key—does he put his clothes back on, or does he take a box-fresh set with him? And what if he forgot to have a shower? He's just slipping on a nice Thomas Pink shirt when—d'oh!—he realizes he smells of chlorine. So he slips off the shirt and his boxers and he has a shower. But when he gets out, does he pop the shirt back on, or does he require a new one? And if he does require a new one and he hasn't got one with him, does he go home in the buff? Or what?

was laced with terms like *mother brand, brand equity,* and *product seeding.* Dash described himself as "a lifestyle entrepreneur. I sell all the time. Whether it's music or sneakers, it's all marketing, marketing, marketing, 24 hours a day. My whole life is a commercial." Clearly these new capitalists are better than the old ones, though. They don't get rich off the backs of others—they do it just by being fly.

Oh, hang on: Ultimate blingster P. Diddy—who produces his own custom-made Sean John diamond-encrusted iPods—destroyed his image as a shrewd businessman in December 2003 when confronted by Lydda Eli Gonzalez, a nineteen-year-old former factory worker from Honduras. She asked him how come the people who made his $50 Sean John T-shirts were paid 24 cents per shirt, limited to two toilet breaks a day, and forced into unpaid overtime. Puffy said he didn't know anything about it. It's okay, though: When he looked into it and discovered what she said to be true, Diddy did right and made sure the factories' conditions were improved. Possibly among the improvements: diamond-encrusting each employee's sewing machine.

For all but a handful, of course, bling is a glaring lie: 50 Cent's 2003 album *Get Rich or Die Tryin'* should more accurately have been called *Highly Unlikely to Get Rich, Far More Likely to Die Tryin'.* But as Public Enemy's Chuck D recently claimed: "Hip-hop is sucking the nipples of Uncle Sam harder than ever before." What he failed to report was how P. Diddy actually manages to suck the nipples of Uncle Sam and his great mate Donald Trump at the very same time. That makes four nipples. But then, as we know, he is quite a guy.

JAMES BLUNT

James Blunt is the perfect singer-songwriter for the busybusy-busy generation who don't have time to consider what a song might actually mean. Literary conceits swallow up valuable minutes that might be spent . . . oh, we don't know, cracking up or having a really massive latte.

Given these constraints, the smartest, sharpest title for a song about a woman being beautiful is surely "You're Beautiful." And why call any song that concerns the pain of saying good-bye to a lover anything other than "Goodbye My Lover"? From this perspective, it's hard to see why anyone gets stewed up about this songwriting game. It's quite straightforward. A fucking monkey could do it.

"Goodbye My Lover" was the emotional core of Blunt's huge-selling debut album *Back to Bedlam.* As the title implies, the song in no way involves saying "hello" to a lover. The situation departs from the pleasures that come with welcoming a lover almost completely. It could equally have been called "Farewell My Lover." Or "See Ya! My Lover."

Blunt—the "epitome of 21st-century chic," according to Britain's *Daily Mail*—has probably said good-bye to quite a lot of lovers. If the tabloids are to be believed, he can't keep it in his trousers: sort of like a posh-rock Charlie Sheen. But those were merely casual lovers. The lyric of "Goodbye My Lover" explores the crucifying angst of losing a woman whom Blunt apparently "pretty much considered the one." Interviewed on *James Blunt at the BBC,* the queen-guarding balladeer called the story "very tragic." And, in many ways, he is right.

The song begins by questioning whether he failed his departed lover, before his thoughts turn back to the early flowering of romance, depicting himself as some sort of victor (that would be the army background, presumably). His powerful presence caused his new lover temporarily to lose her sight. So he decided to take, not forcibly but with a certain righteous zeal, what he considered his property by an everlasting, possibly even divine, covenant. Continuing this reverie, Blunt imaginatively plants his mouth over various parts of his ex-lover's body before recalling how they would both sleep under the same sheets. This is the reason he can then claim intimate knowledge of her physical odor. In the chorus, he repeatedly bids his lover farewell before revealing she was probably the only woman for him in the world. The implication is that he can never love again. That's it. He is spent. Good-bye to love, perhaps.

The second verse finds the war-hero-turned-singer still urgently envisioning his former girlfriend and imploring her to remember him, too. He has watched her at various times, he reveals, while she was crying, while she was smiling, and also while she was sleeping (but not for that long, he also assures her—not so long that it would become fucked up). You see, he would happily have sired offspring with this woman and spent all his born days with her. Actually, you know what? If she isn't there, if she has definitely disappeared for good, then he is genuinely unsure about whether he can carry on living. It's almost "Don't leave me or I'll kill myself!" But it's not quite not that, either. Self-harm, possibly?

The chorus then repeats the claim that she was his only hope. Everything is ruined. And so on. We're nearing the end now, but he must still detail the haunted nights; the nights when, lying in bed, he actually feels her hands. Honestly, it's like she's really there. She's not, though, as we hope we've established.

At the song's climax, he brings out what we have already surmised: that this heartrending experience has left him an empty husk. To emphasize this point, he repeats it six times.

Don't make the mistake of thinking his life has any meaning. Because it hasn't. Okay? Selling lots of records in America? He's not bothered. "People have said it sounds like she died or something like that," he admitted. He's very hunky with his top off and all that. But wouldn't you chuck him, too? The moaning fucktard.

BODY ART

Actually, we think you'll find it's called a *tattoo.* When Picasso painted *Guernica,* it was not, as we understand it, a toss-up between a nightmarish pyramid arrangement of horrors in black, white, and gray representing the effects of fascist bombing, or a big eagle with MOM written underneath it. We could be wrong.

BOOKMAKERS

It is not true what your granny tells you: that no one makes money from gambling and the bookies always win. Very rich people who own horses make money from betting, as they have the information and connections to get on to a good thing. It's old men who hang around in OTBs all day smoking, cheering for horses and dogs in a very quiet, desperate, defeated way, often abbreviating the name as if using the full name of an animal that will, in all likelihood, only cause them pain is just too much for them, who tend not to win.

If bookies look like they're going to lose—that is, loads of people start betting on something that is likely to actually happen—they slash the odds to the point where no one will bother. If that doesn't work, they close the book and stop taking bets. They would call this "sound business sense." We would call this "being a bunch of cunts."

So it's okay to go in to the bookies and say, "I'll put ten bucks on Mystical Dancer in the two thirty. I have it on the excellent authority of a man down the bar that it is a very fast horse indeed, certainly faster than all the other horses in this race, which is, after all, the nub." And they just say, "Okey-dokey, pal." At no point do they say "Mystical Dancer? Cock Dancer, more like. It's a fucking donkey, mate. Save yourself the cash: Unless all the other horses fall over during the race, you haven't got a fuck of a chance. And even then there'd be no guarantee, it's fucking garbage." But if you go in and say, "I'll have one hundred crisp green dollar bills on *Big Bag of Bullshit* by Pompous O'Bastard to win the Booker Prize at 66–1" and some guy in Miami has done the same, and they think you know something they don't and they might lose a few bucks, they say: "Sorry, chief, 66–1? Oh no, that should have read 1–20—slip of the pen—and, erm, anyway we've closed the book for fear we might not make loads of money." Bastards.

BOOKS ON CD (EXCEPT FOR BLIND PEOPLE)*

We may not know much, but we do know this: Books are for reading.

---

* This entry is EXCLUSIVE to the print edition of *Is It Just Me or Is Everything Shit?* The audio book shits on people who waste time reading when they could just listen to it on CD, leaving their hands free for doing jigsaws and eating fudge.

Being read is one of the key characteristics of your actual book. If you don't like reading, you're just not the sort of person who wants to get involved with books. And this isn't rocket science: We learned it in preschool.

The second most insane example of the audio book is the complete *Ulysses* by James Joyce. Now, this is by no means an easy book. It is a very long book—with long words in it and, famously, a really, really fucking long sentence. Not being a booky type, you may decide it's not for you. Fair enough. But what sort of freak who doesn't wish to read *Ulysses* buys the Naxos 22 CD set of someone else reading it for them? You can't be bothered to read it, but you can be bothered to listen to 22 CDs? Freak.

But the first most insane example is *Finnegan's Wake* (also by Naxos), a book that even people who really like reading get frightened of. Indeed, people who like reading so much they do precious little else, who like it so much they majored in Double English Literature with Extra Reading at college just so they could do a shitload of reading, have been known to run off down the street when someone produces a copy of *Finnegan's Wake,* shouting "Stay back! That's too much reading!" For this reason, we firmly believe that all the *Finnegan's Wake* CDs are actually blank.

BOTOX

NewBeauty magazine, dubbed by the *London Times* "The new magazine for the Botox generation," has helpfully collected "40 Uses for Injectables." It's "highly experimental," but Botox can potentially "inhibit the nerve impulses that make you feel hungry." Furthermore, sticking it into the armpit can "completely shut off the production of perspiration." So Botox can save you from sweating or getting the munchies. That's right: just like Barbie.

It's not all post-sweat, post-comestible fun, though. High-powered bankers are injecting Botox to stop looking all frowny and stressed after regularly working eighteen-hour days. One told *Time* magazine: "It's important to look your best . . . like you can take it in your stride."

Of course, injecting yourself with bacteria to look like you're not tired when you really are *very* tired would make you a living metaphor for the age. Which is sort of cool. Hopefully, we're on our way to a big-bosomed, non-frowning utopia. Hey, maybe we should all dye our hair blond and put in blue contact lenses, too? Wouldn't that be perfection?

When the Botox generation dies, what will its ashes look like?

BRATZ

Look, here's saucy leatherclad Roxxi, one of the Bratz Rock Angelz, playing a flying-V rock guitar and showing off her midriff and high heels. Kind of like when Britney dressed up as a Nazi dominatrix. "Hi! My name is Roxxi," says Roxxi. "My twin calls me Spice because I like to spice things up!" Twins, eh? Eh? Wicked!

Bratz are taking over. You might have thought they were just a line of dolls, purple-spangly teenage dolls in "funky" outfits slathered in makeup. But you would be wrong. The Bratz doll is not a doll. Well, it is a doll, anyone can see that. But it's also, according to Paula Treantafelles, who initially created the toys, a "self-expression piece."

How this "self-expression" piece expresses itself is mainly through the prism of having the right trinkets, phones, accessories, and shoes. (Without shoes, the Bratz dolls have no feet. It's kind of a metaphor.) They are "the only girls with a passion 4 fashion!" It's a sort of celebutard training course for six-year-olds.

Doll designer Lui Domingo insists: "We are not making a deliberate effort to sexualize these dolls. We are making them fashionable, and coincidentally the fashions these days are rather sexy." Not trying to sexualize them? They look like a series of Hollywood central casting whores made out of plastic!

Then there's the passion 4 dating guyz: the "Secret Date" range of Bratz includes a dolled-up doll, plus a mystery date (one of the Bratz Boyz) and—oh yes—champagne glasses! Why not go the whole way and chuck them naked into a Jacuzzi? Bubblicious!

Then there are the Bratz Babyz—sort of what babies would look like if they decided to become strippers. And there's a Babyz Night Out fashion pack and Brattoo Parlor playset. Because if there's one thing babies need it's more nightz out and tattoos. They could go out and compare their new markings: "Look, I've got a spider, what about you?" "Mine says 'soul' in Chinese."

Bratz Big Babys (yet another range) have "Designer Diapers"—lovely frilly knickers, which they set off with highly peculiar coquettish poses. Oh yes, and earrings. And a bikini bearing the slogan I BLOW BUBBLES! This is also a coincidence. The fashion among babies is definitely for looking like little sexpots. Oh no, hang on . . . Even the Bratz Babyz Ponyz have colored highlights and makeup. So they're sexualizing ponies now? Come on—if you're sexualizing ponies, you're definitely taking the sexualizing way too far. Or is this a coincidence, too? Are there slave-to-fashion ponies out there now, right this minute, having their tits done?

Hey, we know! How about a Babyz Self-Harm Kit? Or at least just supply the Secret Dates with Rohypnol. Or is that going too far? How does one judge? Anyway, let us be thankful that children are not generally impressionable or easily led—or we may end up with a generation of stifled, consumer-crazed fuckups. Another one.

BRITAIN'S ROYAL FAMILY

All shit.

Well, except for Prince William, whom even we—heterosexual males with strong anti-monarchist beliefs—have to admit to finding so unbelievably beautiful that we almost want to cry. Lord knows, we didn't want this to happen. But just look at him!

Sometimes, we actually find ourselves wondering whether it's love and start spinning involved romantic fantasies in which we both write each other poems and laugh and giggle and laugh some more.

Then, in our darker moments, we can't stop thinking about being taken roughly from behind by Prince Harry dressed as a Nazi.

BROADBAND SERVICE PROVIDERS

While broadband service providers maintain the illusion of competition by vying to have the stupidest name, they actually collude in keeping us in a state of roiling panic.

One day, according to their fiendish plan, you might be up and me down. The next day, the situation might be reversed with me on top, cackling with a glass of something nice, while you're down in the pit feeling abandoned like an abandoned dog feels abandoned when it's been abandoned. Fucked, essentially.

It's the broadband whirligig of life that makes weak, impotent pawns of us all. In fact, when Polish sociology guru Zygmunt Bauman formulated his new theory of the "liquid life," a scary new precariousness that sees the 21st-century individual walking on quicksand, under perpetual siege, while seeking shelter from the storm in Pandora's box (which is on fire), he had just lost his broadband connection and was being seriously dicked around by the helpline staff.

Or is it even more cosmic than this? Is it part of the divine plan, of which broadband companies are mere fucknutted minions? Is there some kind of karmic payback going on? Do we get the broadband service we deserve? Or are we randomly picked out for this torture because we're completely controlled, both physically and metaphysically, by complete bastards? They send our instructions down the broadband cable. It's possible. Well, probably it is—we don't actually understand how it works.

We think it's all of the above. And more.

GEORGE W. BUSH

George W. Bush is much vilified for reasons such as wars, oil, incapacity to eat pretzels without causing injury to himself (the freak), abolishing taxes for the rich, stuff like that—but his critics miss the central, absolutely key point: the fact that George W. Bush claims to "speak Spanish."

Chutzpah? *Hola! ¡Sí!* Fucking hell, *¡sí!* You'd think he'd be better mastering one language at a time, and that English would be a more pressing priority. But *no, señor.* This Hispanic turn is, of course, politically motivated. Here's how it works. In Texas, there are lots of Hispanic voters. So it helps, if you want to be governor of Texas, to get Hispanic people to vote for you. So you "learn Spanish." It's unclear if "speaking Spanish" means he can conduct negotiations with Mexican trade ministers in their native tongue. Or maybe just that he can almost ask his way to the swimming pool—if there's also a mike strapped to his back. But still.

As news of his Latin temperament spread, Bush's share of the Hispanic vote rose from around a third in the 2000 presidential election to 44% in 2004. Kerry (whoever she was) still took 53%, but the gap with the Democrats closed from a 36% deficit in 2000 to 9%—which, as any seasoned election analyst will tell you, is less. If you did some more sums you could predict by how much Bush would lead in the Latino vote next time if he were allowed to run, which he isn't, and it would probably make for scary reading, we should expect. *¡Hola!*

This is why Bush has been sponsoring massive immigration from Spanish-speaking countries—mainly Mexico, which Bush really likes because it rhymes with Texaco, but also Spain itself. That's why Laura delivers leaflets saying "Come to America" outside Mexican wrestling matches. And why the pair of them often hit the Andalusian coastline to swim naked and free. Which, in fact, come to think about it, isn't happening. So, actually, all this stuff about the Spanish thing is wrong and the people who concentrated more on the wars and tax cuts and stuff were right. Sorry.

As Bush's term comes to an end, perhaps we can teach him two more words of Spanish: *"Adios, fuckwit."* Which means: "Bye, President Bush, and thanks for everything you've done for us."

C

CALAMITY PORN

The coffee-table tome of the Apocalypse will look amazing. Certainly, the dry run—*New York September 11,* containing photos of that terrible day taken by the photographers from the illustrious Magnum photo agency—is an eye-catching, one might even say jaw-dropping, document. A vivid memento of one special day to remember.

The 2006 documentary on the Falling Man was built upon the premise that we cannot bear to look upon the image of the midair mystery man jumping to his doom and so end up censoring the image. This was good because it enabled everyone to print the image again, really big, just to prove that we are now brave enough to face the image. Look, here we are: facing it.

Photoshopped images of a future London after some future flood? Horrendous, yes. But also quite cool. After all, didn't New Orleans look dramatic? The picturesque hobos, the battered streets, the martial law surrounding the chain stores . . . and what a soundtrack: Between all the blues and all the jazz, nature could not have wreaked havoc in a more culturally enriching setting.

For years, torture was a very worthy, late-Pinter sort of subject, but now it's family entertainment with pliers-on-body action adding real piquancy to the plots of hip television series like *Lost* and *24*. The whole taboo has really lifted of late: After 9/11, the *New York Times* said that conversations "in bars, on commuter trains, and at dinner tables" were now turning on the relative ethics of torture. It's almost worth a supplement spread: Torture Chic.

"Disaster movies will never be the same again" was one verdict, in the *Guardian,* on *United 93*. Oh, good. So they didn't die in vain. If nothing else, at least we can point to 9/11 as having revived a moribund movie genre. Unfortunately, Nicolas Cage and Michael Peña didn't resurrect the cop buddy movie with Oliver Stone's *World Trade Center,* in which two men bravely fight an evil even worse than Gary Busey in *Lethal Weapon*. Hopefully, other moribund movie genres will also get a twenty-first-century calamity boost. Personally, we can't wait for the first weird weather sex comedy. Or the first post-Guantanamo caper flick.

The acclaim for *United 93* was deafening. Apparently, it was "unifying, and uplifting, at a time when the wars in Iraq and Afghanistan are going badly." Which is, surely, kind of weird. Everything's fucking up! With our governments' efforts to rectify matters only seeming to derectify matters further! But look, here's some proper brave stuff. It's uplifting. More than the nightly news, certainly. We're sick of that stuff.

Of course, artists are beholden to reflect the world around them, and if that involves getting off—in a simplistic way—on the drama of it all, then at least it's not standard-issue Hollywood escapism of rappers in fast cars. Or maybe, in fact, this is the new escapism: seeking respite from the fruitless gloom by getting kicks from bloody, handheld, vérité docudramas on the more horrific flashpoints of the age. "There's so much to see right now. What do you prefer? There's the Twin Towers film or the New Orleans film. Then there's *Fast and Furious: Nightmare in Najaf.* Oh, and *The Taliban Terminator,* about the British sniper in Helmand Province. It's apparently a bit like *Phone Booth*—only they haven't got a functioning telecommunications network."

CARBON OFFSETS

Planting trees: What can possibly be wrong with that? Well, nothing usually. Except if those trees become fig leaves. Fig leaves to help cover up an enviro-hellstorm. Which they won't be able to do. Because fig leaves are small, and enviro-hellstorms are big. The wonder of carbon offsets shows that there really is no problem you can't solve by throwing more money at it, even if that problem is born from having money. Honestly, it's like a little miracle.

So Coldplay can feel okay about the CO_2 emissions of their super-success enormo-gigs by funding the planting of ten thousand mango trees in India. In this way, a recent interview can proudly report the band flying "by private jet to Palm Springs . . . The band can now afford to fly wherever possible." (Of course, pretty soon there might not be any palms or any springs when they fly to Palm Springs—but that won't be their fault!)

In such ways, even an utterly atomized populace can change the world. Any problems? Well, only that it's largely bullshit. The science is disputed, but what is clear is that you cannot even accurately account for the amount of carbon that will be "offset" by planting trees. Trees do temporarily trap some carbon but, unfortunately, they also breathe some of it out again—it's just kind of what they do. (We know this is disturbing, but trees are alive—not like in *Lord of the Rings,* but still . . .) And when the trees are felled, at least some of the carbon will be released back into the atmosphere. So landscape historian Oliver Rackham has compared the practical effect of carbon-offset tree planting to drinking more water to keep down rising sea levels. Even Friends of the Earth, who fucking love trees, say it's "not a solution."

In culinary terms, it's like living on a diet of Big Macs and thinking that's all right because you've also got the slice of tomato, lettuce, and pickle in there. The message is simple: The planet cannot survive on a diet of burgers.

CELEBRITIES TAKING CELEBRITY REALITY TV SHOWS FAR TOO SERIOUSLY

During the filming of *Armed & Famous*—the CBS reality show where celebrities patrolled the mean streets of Munice, Indiana—former *CHiPs* star Erik Estrada said of the experience, "I didn't want to fail so it scared the life out of me."

Don't get so caught up in it, dude. Put it into context: Ponch. A voice on *SeaLab 2021.* Infomercials selling land in Florida. That is *you.*

CELEBRITY FRAGRANCES

Have rubbish names. There's Lovely by Sarah Jessica Parker; David Beckham's Instinct; True Star Gold by Beyoncé; Britney Spears's Fantasy and Britney Spears's Curious. Britney Spears "personifies daring . . . Curious by Britney Spears represents the young woman that pushes boundaries and revels in adventure."

Yes, Britney Spears is indeed fairly curious, although not in the sense that she might suddenly, say, get really into botany. She's curious in a different way. And she's getting curiouser and curiouser.

True Star Gold sounds like one of those obscure gas stations you only ever see in the countryside—like the ones in the industrial part of Burbank with a logo that is almost exactly, although not quite, the same as Exxon's, if Exxon had produced its logo on a Commodore 64.

Sean John's scent is Unforgivable. By which we don't mean it's unforgivable, although it probably is. It's actually called Unforgivable. Apparently, he personally chose the "combination of breathtaking, addictive and slightly dangerous essences." What are "slightly dangerous essences"? Arsenic that's been very heavily diluted? Is Sean John slowly trying to poison the world literally as well as metaphorically now?

Also, why does he always look so miserable? Is he actually miserable?

CELEBRITY MAGAZINES

"She's too *fat*!" "Wait, she's too *skinny*!" "Or is she so utterly *fantastic* it's not true?" "No, she's a *skank*! With sweat stains!"

For fuck's sake, at least make up your minds.

CELEBRITY PRODUCT LINES

In 2004, spotting a gap in the market for credit cards aimed at impressionable teenagers, pop sensation Usher launched his own, sort of like saying, "Hey kids, if you enjoyed my hit album *Confessions,* you'll love a life in debt."

Or if you have a grand to waste, you could get a table designed by Daft Punk covered in different-colored light squares that respond to noise and light up—like a Studio 54–style dance floor. The only point of this is to say rude words to it and see which squares light up.

The queen of celebrity product lines, however, is Suzanne Somers. How committed is she to endorsing stuff? She is so committed that she regularly appears on Home Shopping Network! She is so committed that her short-lived one-woman show on Broadway—no joke—included an infomercial for the ThighMaster! She is so committed that she has stopped being an actual celebrity! True story!

On her Web site, the 1970s' most famous ditzy blonde (not an easy title to win!) sells her own lines of beauty products, fitness products, weight-loss products, books, tapes, jewelry, and apparel. Somers promises she has "carefully selected and tested each item." One can only hope she's currently wearing a lab coat in her R&D department trying out the Suzanne Somers Home Enema Kit.

"CHANGE YOURSELF TODAY!" CULTURE

Understand this: There is something deeply adrift within your personality. Be prepared to chuck it away and start again.

The urge to start afresh seems particularly strong in the New Year. A few hours after the bells have chimed, anyone remaining unaware that they are polluted dipshits will soon be disabused of this by shelves crammed with books offering to Change Your Life in Seven Days. Or possibly Make You Thinner. Or Turn You Inside Out, if That's Your Thing.

Newspaper headlines urge you to "Change Your Life for the New Year: Be Happier, Be Healthier, Be Richer. The Experts Tell You How in Our Special Guide." Why are these writers so obsessed with cleansing their souls and starting fresh? What did they do over Christmas to mire themselves so thoroughly? Did they find themselves shouting racial epithets in the middle of an orgy?

In March 2006, the self-helpish magazine *Psychologies* included a special section called "Get Ready to Change." It had the headline "Are You Ready to CHANGE?" Plus bullet points: "Your life map: what needs to change?" "'How I got a new life'" and "Test: how will you handle change?" A subliminal message arguably emerges here. And it's not: Stay exactly the same as you already are.

A change, it's often said, is as good as a rest. We prefer a rest, ourselves, but there you go. The self is a tricky concept that has been the subject of anguished debate since time immemorial. Maybe the autonomous individual has a burning core of consciousness from which all else exudes. Maybe this is a myth to enforce positive feelings about ourselves and engender the illusion that we can determine our own way in the world. Perhaps we are merely the sum of our socioeconomic relations with other human beings. Or simply the totality of all the words we ever speak and think. Alternatively, we could just be a set of genetically pre-programmed desires designed to propagate the species, a trillion mindless robots dancing . . .

Whatever, it's clearly a tangled affair. So thank the Lord we have Dr. Phil to sort it out.

CHE GUEVARA MERCHANDISE

Let's not be negative about this: Che Guevara did help put in power a Stalinoid dictatorship that locks up gays and trade unionists—but, you know, fair's fair, he did also have a cool beard. And Cuba can't be proper Stalinism, like in Eastern Europe, because it's really sunny there, whereas Eastern Europe is cold. Brr.

Che is everyone's favorite facial-hair-motorbike-stood-for-some-stuff-but-I-don't-know-what-it-was-and-don't-really-give-one-check-out-the-beard-man revolutionary. Awesome. The sort of revolutionary you can safely put on T-shirts, clocks, and candles—yes, Che Guevara candles are available from a firm called Rex International. They also do candles with Elvis on them. Same difference. Che's real name was Ernest, which is perhaps not so cool, but who cares when you factor in the whole motorbike thing?

Or maybe the kids really are into vague, trigger-happy yet hippie-ish developing-world guerrilla vanguard revolutionism tinged with Stalinism? Either way, buoyed up by Rex's success, other companies are trying to float similar products, including a chain of North Korean restaurants full of images of Kim Il Sung (provisionally called Yo! Rice), and a range of sportswear called simply Gulag.

Rex is responsible for Che coasters and the Official Che Guevara calendar. How the red blazes do you get an *official* Che Guevara calendar? Presumably, there is a Guevara estate somewhere sanctioning all this crap? In fact, we've gotten hold of a tape of the chat between Che's relatives and a Rex representative where the historic coasters decision was made:

AUNTIE FLO GUEVARA: It's what he would have wanted.

UNCLE DAVE GUEVARA: Yes, yes. He was always drinking fluids from glasses and mugs, but not all in one go. He needed something to rest the glass or mug on, so as not to mark the surface of the table.

AUNTIE FLO GUEVARA: He was very considerate like that.

UNCLE DAVE GUEVARA: Yes, he was a considerate boy: he always left his machine gun in the hall.

AUNTIE FLO GUEVARA: Yes. And his motorbike.

UNCLE DAVE GUEVARA: Yes, the motorbike also.

AUNTIE FLO GUEVARA: How much money were you going to give us again?

UNCLE DAVE GUEVARA: Yes, we need to pay our gardener in the Maldives. We haven't lived in Cuba for years—it's shit. They lock up gays, you know.

AUNTIE FLO GUEVARA: Yes, and glasses and mugs—they just put them on the table. Just right on the table. They don't even care if it makes a mark!

UNCLE DAVE GUEVARA: They're animals. Cigar?

DICK CHENEY

Sometimes, one may have doubts about whether it's right to demonize one man as the figurehead for all gas-guzzling, planet-raping, profiteering bastardry. We might momentarily wonder whether such a complex individual can really be so baldly drawn as the pure, living embodiment of bug-eyed Republican evil. Then, for a relaxing day off, he gets buzzed and shoots another man in the face.

Dick Cheney hunts pensioners—releasing them into the Texas scrubland, then letting off 260 pellets of leaden injury right in their faces. Still, at least it gets him into the outdoors—his previous exercise having been confined to climbing greasy poles and counting his money.

Cheney has often been called the architect of the Iraq War (however, an architect would have made a plan—so let's just say it was "his fault"). Even people supposedly on his side (Lawrence Wilkerson, a former aide to Colin Powell) have openly wondered whether his propensity to ignore UN conventions makes him a war criminal. His enemies, however, *really* don't like him.

After the shooting, Cheney took awhile to take responsibility for pumping buckshot into hapless Harry Whittington. It was a full fourteen hours before the cops were called. Earlier, the local sheriff—alerted to the incident by the call made to the ambulance service—had been turned away from the estate by security guards who "knew of no incident." According to our sources, the full fourteen hours were taken up with an in-depth debate on how to play the issue. Cheney argued that if he could get Whittington classified as an "unlawful enemy combatant" then he could not only shoot him in the face but also torture him. "Let's waterboard the fucker," Mr. Cheney is reported as saying. He then suggested the excuse "An Arab did it." Ultimately, his final gambit that he should "privatize responsibility" having fallen on deaf ears, he was persuaded to go on TV and claim to be "a bit sorry."

Even then, he managed to turn his admission that he shot an old man in the face—"I'm the guy who pulled the trigger that fired the round that hit Harry"—into a piece of singsong circumlocution in the style of "There Was an Old Lady Who Swallowed a Fly."

We don't know why she swallowed a fly. But we strongly suspect part of the reason Dick Cheney didn't alert the police until fourteen hours after he had pulled the trigger that fired the round was because he was an old man who had swallowed a beer. Followed by another beer. Possibly to catch the first beer. Who knows?

CHICK LIT

Competition: Three of the below chick-lit titles are real chick-lit titles and two are not real but made-up chick-lit titles. Can you spot the not real but made-up ones? (Answers below.)

1. *Dot.Homme:* Midthirties singleton Jess is sent by friends into the world of Internet dating—with unexpected results!
2. *The Ex-Files:* Take a soon-to-be-married young couple, four exes, mix with alcohol, and stand well back. Boom!
3. *Virtual Strangers:* Fed up, frustrated, and fast approaching forty, Charlie suddenly thinks she may have finally found her perfect soul mate—via e-mail!
4. *The Mile High Guy:* Twentysomething Katie is a flight attendant thrown head over heels by a handsome, wealthy first-class passenger. Emergency landing!
5. *Old School Ties:* Tracey is thirty-two, married, and bored. Then she spies an ad for a reality show on a perfect school reunion. Friends—and enemies—are soon reunited!

Answers: Sadly, there are no answers.

CHINESE COMMUNIST PARTY, THE

Peasants, the blind tide who have floated down rerouted rivers, hanging off girders a hundred thousand stories high. Everything everywhere expanding like a great big expanding thing that moves very quickly. In 1998, sixteen of the world's twenty most polluted cities. We must build more. Build more and capture the last few places until the buildings eat the sky. Wonders accomplished far surpassing Roman aqueducts, Gothic cathedrals, the Burj Al Arab. No one can breathe. It doesn't matter.

Everyone must live in a pod hotel and eat out. All the restaurants in China full—all the Chinese restaurants full of Chinese people, which, as we know from our dads, is "always a good sign." Now twenty-four million chickens eaten a day. It's not enough. Soon they won't be able to wait, and will just eat the eggs. Everything laced with agricultural chemicals and animal hormones: women buying tits; men growing them. "Western" technology bought or taken. A resplendent Olympics showcasing the all-new Reeducation Through Labor event. Beijing sites of English public schools churning out Chinese public schoolboys. Polo. Party princelings and the rich renew their organs from slaughtered-to-order cultists and Christians. Power brokers chasing "wild flavors" gorge on SARS-carrying civet cats from the wild animal markets of southern China. Businessmen's prandial panda penises wreak disease and pestilence in foreign financial centers that are no longer houses of finance but merely houses of whores. Kids sent away to see how estate agents live. Kids who now can read but cannot read their history. *Teen Vogue* swearing allegiance to the party. No longer an iron smelter in every garden—steel plants for all that want them, dismantled and labeled piece-by-piece and shipped in from Germany. Motorways upon motorways—leading inevitably to motorway service stations; corrupt officials skimming off the top to leave potholes and cave-ins for unwary capitalist drivers. Families hitherto forced to work at opposite ends of the country now can work at opposite sides of the globe. A mature society, with proper vast inequality between the super-rich and the super-poor.

They will solve the problems of the countryside by abolishing the countryside. All will be a constantly renewing urban sprawl, an end of days of peasants starving while they feed the cities; now they can starve in the cities—cities leaping through stages of development and redevelopment. And again. A billion five-car families buying wide-screen refrigerators. A billion coal-fired arms dealers propping up revolving African despots. Socialism that you cannot eat becoming state capitalism that you cannot stop eating. Obesity: growth measured with a tape measure around the waist.

Production-producing product producers nestle everywhere, settle everywhere, establish connections everywhere. The cheap prices of Chinese commodities are the heavy artillery with which the new system batters down all Chinese walls, bringing home brands as souvenirs. Baby milk. Toys and tractors. Soft war by penicillin production. If only we could make the West wear its shirttails half an inch longer; the mills of China would be working around the clock. The world gorged on cheapness. Wal-Mart merrily marking up marks-ups that merely mark the end. The West desiccated and ruined—everyone reduced to surviving by selling one another their knickknacks on eBay and servicing one another. The rest of the time is spent falling down manholes, the iron caps melted as scrap by kids to send east. Kids once more display posters of Mao. The only good goods the Chinese goods.

Fish, wood, logs legal and illegal. Oil. Wood for wood; wood to make way for soybeans. 20% of the population; 7% of the arable land. Raw materials sucked in from the globe like a giant fishing factory-ship draining all the oceans at once, commodity prices trebling even in the instant that they are sold. Norwegian men fight in the street like dogs, over tree saplings. The West morally outraged by the combination of low wages and environmental degradation. The very idea! Taiwan purchased. A yo-yo of African despots, misery revolving; cash loans and ivory palaces bestowed upon the new dictators. China Radio International broadcasting as Radio Not Free Nairobi. But starvation-waged copper miners listen instead for accidents. More Chinese in Nigeria than the Brits ever had. Hard power. Oil wars. Chinese fiefdoms in the Middle East—Mad Max beyond the Terrordome. Mel Gibson strung up on an oil derrick like Christ.

Jailed journalists fail to report the unveiling of the statue of the Google founders—1,989 feet high at the gates of the Forbidden City, next to the mural of Mao. Under it, the Google motto—now the organizing principle of the Communist Party of China—DO NO EVIL. Kids jailed for Internet searching "Tiananmen." Twenty years for throwing an egg. Shi Tao—jailed for ten years for e-mailing abroad how the paper he worked for covered the fifteenth anniversary of the slaughter in the square. Yahoo! helped identify him. Yahoo!/Google/Microsoft: Will you let me search "police informants" or "accomplices to repression"? Murdoch: He knows a ruthless money-hungry elite when he sees one. Seek truth from facts—even if you have to make them up.

Party and nation fused; run by arse-lickers, nepotistic yes-men, and old-fashioned bastards. Lawless local government mafias getting fat on the wages of migrants, siphoning enviro-cash to build coal-fired coal burners, just for kicks, state loans disappearing in a puff of sulfurous smoke. Close to two hundred thousand party members found guilty of corruption in 2004—just the careless ones. Grasping at the organs of the living—imprisoned for the fear of funny-exercising Falun Gong. Churches putting party before God in their screeds. The organs of Christians (body organs, not big music ones with pipes—that would be stupid). The organs of the trade unionists. The organs of those jailed for having a picture of the Dalai Lama: Look, he's "Tibetan."

Tiananmen? An "incident." The Cultural Revolution? A couple of mistakes may have been made. Thirty million dead of famine? We couldn't possibly comment. We prefer to be called the ruling party, as if someone else might get a go.

Acid rain already falling in Canada reaches all the way around the world and comes back. But it cannot be enough. Overproduced stockpiles of baby clothes tower. Workers handed the shitty stick—and are then struck with it if they strike. The iron rice bowls are empty. A communist state that is not as socialist as Germany—spending less than half the share of GDP on its people. One hundred twenty million migrant workers with no welfare. Housing sold off. Mass state layoffs. Releasing private firms from the commitment to fund health care and workers' kids' education. But it cannot be enough. Beating back social movements like bashing moles with a mallet. No one can stop this? There are 1.3 billion

Chinese who need to consume like Americans. There is no alternative? The Three Gorges Dam—the world's most costly construction project, its opponents disappeared? "It is not enough! I want a bigger dam! Get me more gorges!"

Onward. Driving up commodity prices until you have to pay to stand in the breeze. Everyone is eating everything, and everyone is being eaten. Everyone waiting for the Chinese Elvis. But she is in the army. A billion boys and girls, no longer aborted, playing video games continuously for days on end. Once, kids denounced their parents. Now parents bottle pressure up in kids. The kids lose themselves in online games; generations jump from buildings, believing they can live and die and live again, as in a game. But you cannot repair nature. The air is like sewage. But what do you want? Scenery or production? All relationships are burst asunder except relations to money and relationships to the party. Ancient traditions prove futile to resist and are swept away. New traditions are ratified unanimously by the National People's Congress. All that is holey is propaned. A man stands stripped bare in a dry riverbed, clutching a pirate Harry Potter with an alternative ending. Everyone is melting.

Well, that's one school of thought, anyway. Who knows? Maybe sense will prevail. Or they might just run out of oil or get tired or something.

CLASSICAL RELAXATION ALBUMS

No one's interested in listening to classical music for the exciting bits anymore. Dark, doomy symphonies evoking a Europe awash with revolution and romantic spirits tussling with their demons, eventually climaxing with some big fuck-off cannons going off all over the place? No thanks, we've only just finished our Boston Market dinner. And we've lit some candles.

Beethoven's Symphony no. 9, with its tormented lows and ravishing highs, was all right back in the day. But never in a million years could it fit into a classical relaxation compilation, advertised with an announcer cooing in weirdly over-sensual tones, like he's spent all his voice-over money on exotic candles and jelly: "Relaxing . . . classical . . . music . . . mmmm . . . mmmmm."

Silly old Ludwig. If only he'd stuck to that balming rinkydink stuff that's like sipping a cool glass of yoga, he might have saved himself a whole lot of bother. Shame, because he really must have put himself out. What with being stone deaf and all.

BILL CLINTON

Whenever the Democrats need to add some glamour, they wheel out Bill Clinton. These days, Clinton is seen as the last great "progressive" U.S. president, the 1990s Good Guy who stands up for fine, admirable things like books. But Clinton's primary loyalties were always to the people dishing out the campaign dosh, like the auto and gun industries. And how progressive was his flagship pledge to "end welfare as we know it"—which he did not by overhauling the meager benefits system to favor the neediest, but instead by quite literally *ending* welfare, canceling the benefits of pregnant women who didn't take low-paying jobs? About as progressive as someone cleaning the wax out of your ears with a soldering iron.

Clinton's New Democrats even invented a new political

word, "triangulation," to denote using progressive rhetoric to pacify voters while continuing to do the bidding of big business. But really, two old words would have sufficed: "telling" and "lies."

CNN, NBC, ETC.

Who would have thought, when the concept of the global media first appeared, that what they meant was the whole globe getting *American* media? Really, *who* could have predicted that?

And why are they always called Bob? The bloke doing the piece to camera in Washington? Bob. Who hands back to the studio—to Bob. Sometimes it's women. But mostly it's Bob.

We once saw this on CNN:

BOB: A flood in Indo- Indo- . . . how do you say that, Bob?
BOB: Inda Indakinesia.
BOB: a flood in Indostania has left four hundred people dead with another thousand so far unaccounted for. But first, let's go back to Minneapolis to get an update on that dog up a tree. She's a real cutey, too. Bow wow, Bob.
BOB: Bob. Bow wow.

When we say we *saw* this, we had been drinking so it might not have happened. In case you were going to use it in an essay or something. Or work as a lawyer for CNN.

They definitely did call forces fighting the United States in Fallujah "anti-Iraqi forces," though. And you can check that. You can't fucking touch us for that one—so don't even try. We were on vacation. It was August 2004. Not sure which day it was. They had CNN where we were staying. You might wonder what we were doing inside watching CNN when we should have been outside in the sunshine enjoying our time off. But it was the evening.

COLORS OF THE SEASON

Who actually decides the new colors of the season? Is it God? No, it's not. It's actually a global network of analysts and trend forecasters in organizations like the Color Association of the United States (CAUS) and Pantone, Inc., who together form a kind of new black Bilderberg Group. They meet in secret, possibly in Davos, possibly in a high-tech base built into a volcano, and usually let the weakest links in the group—possibly those with a distasteful penchant for lime green—take their chances down the shark chute. Their forecasts influence designers of shirts, paper products, candles, cars, tiles, paints, silk flowers, and lipstick. When they say "Aqua," the rest of the world says, "How high?" These people know about color. The CAUS Web site boasts: "Pinks and fuchsia were everywhere in spring 2003; CAUS members knew this in spring of 2001." That's some serious knowledge.

But predicting colors is a strange pursuit—a bit like predicting cows. Basically, they're just kind of there; not really getting any better or worse with the passage of time. This partly explains why, describing their recent aqua-blue ranges, designers Narciso Rodriguez and Michael Kors could only really claim inspiration from seeing—surprise!—some blue water.

"Color is always out there," pointed out Leatrice Eiseman, executive director of the Pantone Color Institute, to *Time* magazine. "We just have to determine where it's coming from at any given time."

Beware of flying color. It's "out there."

COMEDY CLUBS

In every comedy club chain, the MC always kicks off with the lie: "We've got a great bill for you tonight." His icebreaking banter involves asking the audience where they have come from. Perhaps inevitably, the answers rarely provoke high comedy, so the conversation very soon starts resembling distant relatives who haven't met for many years exchanging pleasantries at a funeral: "So where did you come from?" "Mineola." "Great."

The first act begins by explaining that he's "trying out new material." Sadly, though, somewhere in his mind the phrase *new material* has become entirely disassociated with the concept of "jokes." Fairly soon, it goes so quiet you can hear people pissing in the toilet.

After a few more minutes of no jokes, a bachelor party starts yelling: "Fuck off, you suck." "No," the comedian shouts back, "you fuck off." When this has finished, the host returns to try simultaneously to convey the two sentiments "Don't do that or I'll have to get tough" and "Please, for the love of God, do not turn on me."

This pattern is repeated three or four times until the arrival of the headliner—or, rather, the pseudo-headliner, the actual headliner having canceled (a fact advertised by a small handwritten note stuck on a wall behind a curtain). The bachelor party's "fuck offs" will grow in intensity until you realize, as they trade unamusing insults with another bastard working through their "issues" by inflicting their paper-thin personality on people who have never done anything to hurt them, that you have paid good money to sit in a dark room listening to people bellow "fuck off" at one another.

COPPOLAS: THE NEXT GENERATION

The portrait of the babbling airhead Hollywood star in *Lost in Translation* was reportedly based upon writer-director Sofia Coppola's firsthand experience of Cameron Diaz. We would personally be very interested to see Cameron Diaz make her directorial debut with a movie that featured a supercilious rich-kid indie *auteur* who does pseudo-profound confections that people initially splooge themselves over but which, on second viewing, are the cinematic equivalent of unflavored rice cake, with comedy scenes that are not especially funny, endless "arty" shots of the Tokyo skyline filmed out of hotel windows, and dialogue that is only naturalistic in the sense that it possibly took as long to write as to say, and which are considered original only by people who have never set eyes on any other footage showing characters suffering from exquisitely well-turned neon-lit urban ennui like Wim Wenders directing a crap U2 video in 1993.

And she was shit at acting.

Still, at least Sofia creates movies based on her own navel-gazing. Brother Roman Coppola and cousin Jason Schwartzman are content to simply gaze at Wes Anderson's navel, who himself is twee enough to be named an honorary Coppola Jr. These guys are your go-to trio if you want a legitimately interesting subject (like, say, India's native culture) seen through the patronizing eyes of bored, rich white guys. While listening to the Kinks. If they joined forces with Sofia, the resulting film would be so precious that even the most pretentious, clove-smoking art school student would be screaming out, "Cheer the fuck up, nerds!"

And come to think of it, Nicolas "Cage" Coppola hasn't made a decent movie in years. And his hair fell out. So think on.

COSMETIC SURGERY GONE WRONG AS TELEVISION ENTERTAINMENT

Permanent scarring: Now, *that's* television.

CREATIVE INDUSTRIES, THE PHRASE

Funny how you never hear novelists or painters say they work in the "creative industries," but only squalid little advertising people. How could this be?

J. Walter Thompson, the world's oldest ad agency—founded in 1864, it currently handles Ford and Unilever—tells us on its Web site: "We believe: in influencing the world to think more creatively." Provided, presumably, that thought is *Must—buy—more—stuff.*

If you listen to advertisers, you'd think they're the fucking Oracle and that for a fee they'll slip you The Answer. They are obsessed with being seen as "creative," but what they do seems rather to be "parasitical": pinching cultural innovations and using them to persuade people that they want stuff. So there's a dilemma right there for us all to think "creatively" about.

JWT also believes in "raising the creative bar as far as it

will go. Then jacking it up a notch after that." However, having already raised the creative bar as far as it will go, further notching up the creative bar will cause the creative bar to break. The creative bar will be completely fucked. That's just physics.

J. Walter Thompson further believes: "90% of the world's surface is made up of ideas. The rest is water." A brief look at an atlas or infants' school geography textbook could have disabused them of this errant fallacy. Creative? Maybe—after all, they have completely made it up. But certainly not "industrious."

Leo Burnett (which does Heinz and McDonald's) is also into "belief": "We believe Disney, McDonald's, Nintendo, Heinz and Kellogg's are some of the world's most valuable brands because people have gone well beyond merely buying them. These are brands people believe in. When people believe, they buy more, pay more, stick with a brand more and advocate the brand to others. And so belief is the ultimate brand currency."

Instead of all this gibberish about creative bars and making wine from water, really to convey the essence of their activities they'd all be better off with just one page of flashy swirly graphics, fading in these five words:

We

are

emperors

of

shit

CRITICAL REASSESSMENT

Yes, for fuck's sake. By which we don't mean yes, as in "the affirmative." We mean no—to Yes.

In their lifetime, the prog rockers were critically reviled and were held in particular derision by the punk movement. There was a reason for this: They were so bad they made your ears want to die. However, having tried to wreck completely all music by making really bad music is no barrier to critical reassessment, the process in which rock critics look for a date on a CD, see 1973, and think: "Hmmmmmmm, interesting . . ."

The criteria for critical reassessment reflect the high critical standards traditionally exercised by the music press. The criteria are:

- You must once have put a record out.
- Erm, that's it.

You might imagine that revisiting 1980s-era Genesis in a lavish five-CD, five-DVD box set (including remastered albums, rarities, outtakes, and a photo gallery of "rare tour memorabilia") has scraped through the bottom of the barrel into the dark, dirty ground. But even now a few neglected cases are still, in our humble opinion, ripe for rediscovery:

- Solo albums by members of Guns N' Roses.
- Salt-N-Pepa—*The Later Years.*
- The George Martin stuff on side two of the original 1969 release of the *Yellow Submarine* album (which nobody has actually ever listened to).
- Ashlee Simpson—*The Kindergarten Demos.*

- Gary Cherone–era Van Halen.
- U2.

TOM CRUISE

Writing a piece for *Time* magazine on "The People Who Shape Our World," Tom Cruise waxed miracle about *Mission: Impossible 3* director J. J. Abrams: "It's hard to convey with brevity the extraordinary experience of knowing and working with J. J. Abrams. First of all, is there anything in a name—J. J.? Look at the Jays we have now—Jay Leno, J.Lo, Jay-Z—but he's got two J's. He was born to impinge and invade pop culture."

There are many reasons to fear Tom Cruise. There's his fully functioning World War II fighter plane. The way he thinks all psychological problems can be cured by "vitamins and exercise" (he might himself consider a brisk walk down to Whole Foods). There's all that stuff about the silent birth thing. Those films. But given that he believes we are descended from super-intelligent aliens (see *Xenu*), it is perhaps not wholly surprising that when he turns his hand to journalism, the results are utterly off their head and, well, look like they have been written by an alien.

Anyway, Cruise finished his lavish eulogy by revealing that J. J. is a "loving husband to his beautiful wife Katie (can you believe this coincidence?) and father of three glorious children. Gotta give it up for that J2."

Can we believe that Abrams, like Cruise, also has a wife called Katie? Well, yes. Super-aliens: no. Two women being called Katie: We're not feeling that to be too much of a stretch. It's quite a common name: Katie Couric, Katey Sagal, KT Tunstall, Katie, the California Angels Rally Monkey. That's four more, right there.

CULTURE OF PRAISE, THE*

As in, when describing an unremarkable work of artistic creation, the application of words like *magnificent, unbelievable, an awesome achievement,* and *If you don't think this is unfathomably great, I'm coming back with my rifle and the two of us are going to teach you some sense.* Are these bringers of hyperbole being paid in sacks of gold? Or are they the subjects' moms in disguise? According to these throwers of garlands, we live in an unparalleled age where a new masterpiece is being created by another genius roughly every twenty seconds as opposed to, say, every other year.

If book reviewers like a book they've been given, they often claim it is "hard to put down." Has anyone else except book reviewers ever noticed this phenomenon? Some books are even "dare-to-put-me-down" books. Soon we will be faced with "if-you-put-me-down-I'll-rip-your-fucking-feet-off" books. And then where will we be?

Hanging from awnings outside theaters, a succession of boards cherrypick key phrases like *awe-inspiring, unspeakably moving, pure brilliance,* and *a courageous step into the void.* It's surprising audiences aren't struck deaf, dumb, or blind by their experiences. At the very least they should have pissed themselves.

Speaking of pissing yourself, actresses like Kate Winslet often find themselves referred to as "brave." When recently asked by veteran CBS reporter Tom Fenton about being "an uncompromising, very brave actress," Winslet replied: "Being brave is

---

* One literary critic called this entry "Truly stupendous—a work of unparalleled greatness. It actually made me aroused. I'd be very surprised if the authors didn't cure cancer. Just by looking at it."

very important because sometimes, you know, you can find yourself in scary situations at work, you know, when there are scenes that are difficult to do. And you can't run away from it, so you just have to go headlong into it."

We must all applaud Kate Winslet's ability to cope with scary situations at work. But, we must also wonder, how brave is she really? It would be intriguing to see how she'd hold up faced with the challenge of, say, a burning orphanage.

Watching her go headlong into that would indeed be "awesome."

D

DANCE MUSIC AS THE FUTURE

In the 1990s, many people thought dance music was The Future of Music and the Future of Everything; that catching a few DJ sets by Paul Oakenfold would eventually forge young people together as The Oneness—a single bubbling, bouncing organism strong enough to move any mountain. Although why you would want to move mountains is beyond us. Moving a mountain is the sort of project you would only embark upon if you were completely off your meds.

These days, dance music's main function is to provide excuses to wear robot costumes (Daft Punk), mash up hits of the 1970s and '80s (Girl Talk), and help Damon Albarn find reasons not to record a new Blur album (Gorillaz).

And that is the story of dance music.

DEAD PROSTITUTES

Why are all TV crime thrillers centered on dead prostitutes? Jesus, prostitution must be fairly tough already, without some hack bumping you off every ten minutes. We're surprised there are any left. And it's not even enough for them to be "dead." Most of them also have to be "mutilated."

Cold Case, Without a Trace, Dexter, CSI, CSI: Miami, CSI: New York, CSI: Cleveland . . . plus all the *Law & Orders,* especially *Special Victims Unit.* Whenever the *SVU* writers run out of "ripped from the headlines" rape cases, you can bet Belzer and Ice T are gonna discover another dead hooker.

And it's not just on the boob tube, or in this case the blue-nippled, rigor-mortised boob tube. In movies, there are only two types of prostitutes: dead ones, and ones with a heart of gold. And if you glance at any crime/thriller book reviews—especially for the latest by James Patterson, who's a literary Jack the Ripper—and you'll likely find: "Dr. Tony Hill is a clinical psychologist whose assistance is often sought by Detective Carol Jordan, with whom he conducts a hesitant waltz of the 'will they/won't they?' variety. The mutilated body of a prostitute has been found." Has it? No shit.

DELICATESSEN COUNTERS AT SUPERMARKETS

The pasta salads piled up in those quaint earthenware bowls are, of course, produced by the Italian matriarch up to her elbows in prosciutto out back, merrily crushing her own spices while joshing with the French peasant crafting his authentic cheese.

Either that, or they've been mass-produced, loaded into plastic containers, transported across the country in a big lorry, removed from the plastic containers, and placed into said earthenware bowl to seem just ever so slightly more appealing than the absolutely identical ones in vacuum-sealed plastic multipacks on the shelves.

That pasta salad? They've just cooked some pasta and then let it go cold. I will not take a number. I am a free man.

DESIGNER BABY CLOTHES

NEW DAD: Hey, here's an idea—let's get the baby a monogrammed Ralph Lauren polo for $50 that it'll probably grow out of tomorrow afternoon.

NEW MOM: Great. Do they do baby socks in, like, gold thread? That'd be good.

NEW DAD: Yes, it's so important to dress the baby right—you know, to dangle wealth off it.

NEW MOM: Mmm. Otherwise, what's the point?

NEW DAD: Maybe we could get a head-to-toe outfit from Moschino? Is that what Tim and Candelabra got for little, erm, baby? Or was it DKNY?

NEW MOM: Tricky. What would Gwyneth do? Oh, and then there's I Pinco Pallino! They're Italian, so that's some educational value right there.

NEW DAD: And what about those $1,000 Silver Cross strollers? *I want one!* I mean . . . the baby wants one.

NEW MOM: Fucking awesome, yeah!

NEW DAD: We could pimp it up real good—jack up the wheels, get some 26-inch rims on those babies, some leopardskin goin' down . . . Cristal, pick up some bitches . . . ooh, yeah! I'm all excited . . . I think I'll put the Jay-Z CD on.

NEW MOM: Um, darling, you know what? I've been thinking . . . I'm actually quite bored with the baby now—I mean, we've had it for, like, eight weeks or something. Maybe we could drop it off at a Salvation Army or something? Like with shoes.

DICTIONARY SERVICES FOR TEXT MESSAGING

Dictionaries: not exactly in the spirit of the texting age. If these mobile dictionary services are meant as an enticement to stick strictly to the rules of the language, they conspicuously are not working.

Or maybe they're there to inspire greater linguistic flourishes when working out where to meet up and who has been doing what to whom. In which case, maybe we could fit other great reference tomes onto our mobile phones—like dictionaries of quotations for when the time has come to stand on the shoulders of the giants of erudition.

"I believe it was aphorist and clergyman Charles Caleb Colton who first said, 'Wen u hav nutn 2 say, say nutn :)"

"Gr8"

DIDDY DAY

Anyone still wondering whether America's moral code has gone through some particularly rusty scrambler should consider that Las Vegas has now instituted May 14 as Diddy Day, a special day to commemorate that latter-day Martin Luther King, P. Diddy. "Our hope is that he continues to bring his electrifying presence to Las Vegas," said Mayor Oscar Goodman.

What he might have done instead was to declare May 14 as Dido Diddy Diddy Dodo Day—a special day dedicated to the female singer-songwriter, the "electrifying" urban music mogul, and the extinct flightless bird formerly native to Mauritius. We're not saying that would have been better, but it would have been different. A bitch to organize, though.

DISASTER RELIEF DISASTERS

When it comes to disasters, Western governments are like drunk uncles: forever making wild promises they have no intention of keeping.

When Hurricane Mitch devastated Central America in 1998, nearly $100 billion was pledged by governments, but only 33% was ever delivered. After floods struck Mozambique in 2000, $439 million was pledged by governments—but only $219 million, or around half, was delivered.

Most startling is the fact that, of the $1.1 billion pledged after the Bam earthquake in Iran in 2003, only $17 million ever turned up. That's 2%. That's one seriously drunk uncle talking some serious drunk shit about taking you to the zoo and stuff.

"We never get all the money we are pledged," says Elizabeth Byrs of the UN's Office for the Coordination of Humanitarian Affairs. As well as simply not paying up, governments also pull neat accounting tricks like diverting money that was to go to other needy situations, or making a big fuss of suspending affected countries' debt repayments but all the while allowing the interest to mount up, so when the country does start repaying it has a ginormous sum to pay back.

Harry Edwards, a spokesperson for USAID, the U.S. government agency responsible for distributing humanitarian and economic assistance funds, said: "A lot of countries don't pay. The United States isn't the only one." He later claimed that, anyway, a bigger boy made him do it.

Another trick is to count money spent on the military, which may offer assistance, as part of the total. That is, use the disaster as a way of subsidizing the military, recouping military expenditure from your supposed charitable donation. Is there nothing the U.S. will not milk to fund the military? We're surprised there aren't neo-cons wandering round the White House looking for stuff to melt down: "This big stamp and the pad—the one with the eagle on it—do we actually need this? We do? Okay. What about this picture of Abraham Lincoln? No one remembers who the fuck he was anyway, let's put it on eBay."

Of course, even when the money is paid, there's no guarantee it'll actually help the victims. Take, for example, the most fucked up of all motherfuckers, Hurricane Katrina. Following the disaster, the U.S. State Department received $126 million from thirty-six countries and international organizations. One year later, *Foreign Policy* checked in to see how that money was spent and found that $66 million was allocated to FEMA, which then gave it to the nonprofit arm of the United Methodist Church, which distributed almost none of the money to Katrina evacuees. During those critical first 365 days afterward, the nonprofit disbursed only $13 million of the money, and that mostly to pay employee salaries. Because nobody should help homeless hurricane victims for free.

Oh, and as for the remaining $60 million of that international aid? It languished for over six months in a non-interest-bearing account at the U.S. Treasury, before being signed over to the Louisiana Department of Education, which one year later—can you guess the next few words?—had yet to spend a dime! Listen, teachers, we know you guys aren't used to seeing money, but please, share it with the entire class.

DOCTORS

In June 2005, a UK documentary offered a compelling reason why so many general practitioners manage that trademark double whammy of talking in slow, patronizing tones while also being utterly hopeless in the actual "helping people" department: They are either drunk or high on drugs.

Or rather, one in fifteen of them is, anyway. The others are just pricks.

DOCTORS ON DAYTIME TV

There's something that doesn't really scream Hippocratic ideals about being paid cartloads of cash for sitting around on a sofa chatting about hysterectomies. Also, they're always so fucking nice to everyone, which makes us think they can't possibly be real doctors.

PETE DOHERTY BLOOD PAINTINGS

Romantic rock rebel, Kate Moss enabler, and poet Pete Doherty speaks to his generation. And what he mainly says is: "Give me some money so I can go and buy some crack with it. I'm literally crackers . . . for crack!"

When Doherty was imprisoned for his various cracky crimes, UK newspapers ran extracts from his prison diaries: "I'm an innocent man. Wiggy only goes and gives me a stretch in chokey! Oh, my stars, the curdled days of toil and distress—lay me down my rivers of blue chalk and tears. And that."

Doherty has famously broken down the historic barrier between musician and fan. Sometimes, he does this by removing blood from fans' veins with which he then produces useless paintings for his Web site. In response to pictures of him seeming to inject an unconscious girl with heroin, he revealed that he was only taking blood from the girl's arm for another painting—kind of the blood painter's equivalent of running down to

Pearl for some more watercolors. He wrote on his site: "The photos are stolen from my flat so . . . upsetting and personally catastrophic . . . how rude, secondly it's a staged shot and what a fucking liberty to suggest I'd bang up a sleeping lass."

Yes, how rude. Says the man who went down for burgling his best friend's flat. Of course, removing someone's blood while they lie on the floor for a blood painting is the height of modern etiquette.

Doherty has famously built back up the historic barrier between musician and fan by failing to turn up to many of his own gigs. Asked about this by *NME* magazine, he explained: "Yeah? In what sense did I miss gigs? Missed them as in fondly missing them? I didn't miss any fucking gigs."

When the *NME* pointed out that he'd "missed" them in the sense of "not turning up," Doherty countered: "And who did? Who did? Who did turn up? Let them show their faces. What do they want, blood?"

Well, we know he's got some.

But maybe there is hope. During a 2005 *NME* interview, he refused to speak to the journalist until he gave him money to score drugs. He then jumped on the *NME* hack and tickled him and coercively removed his jacket because he liked it, then suggested that the journalist's drink had been spiked with acid, then boasted about head-butting someone. By July 2006, he just wanted to tell the *NME* about his exciting new direction. So he's moving away from drab mumbling of dull nonsense over listless strumming to . . . rap.

So, rap, then. Oh, and—wait for it—reggae. Thankfully, here in the United States, we'll never hear any of it. "Kate Moss's crackhead boyfriend makes music? I thought he just smoked crack!"

DUBAI

We've seen the future and it works! Well, with the help of slave labor it works, anyway.

Through a combination of ambition, sunshine, not levying taxes, and old-fashioned lunacy, Dubai has turned itself into the fantasy-world holiday destination of the age, offering ample parking, shopping, and money-laundering opportunities on the side. There are underwater hotels plus the world's tallest building, and the whole thing is being run off slave labor. It's what Vegas would be like if it had any kind of gumption at all. Have you seen all the amazing things going on over there? It's almost like, only eight hundred miles away from the chaos in Iraq, there's this awesome, glittering haven that's . . . well, it's chaos, too—but mighty fine chaos.

The new opportunities and cheap flights are attracting people of all descriptions: 15 million of them visited Dubai in 2005, of which the largest single group were the Brits (650,000 of them). Richard Branson has an island there; Gordon Ramsay has opened a new restaurant; David Beckham, Posh Spice, and her implants have a villa. This dusty, quite deserty garden of earthly delights has become our closest terrestrial equivalent to those casino-planet pit stops the Starship *Enterprise* was forever stopping off at in the original *Star Trek:* a place where all species can kick back and where Captain Kirk's eye will be caught by a woman with big hair and blue skin before the facade cracks to reveal the kingdom's dark secret . . .

In Dubai, being big is big. The most famous landmark is the sail-shaped Burj Al Arab hotel, the world's only self-styled *seven*-star hotel built on its own man-made island with a helipad on the 28th floor. Everything is covered in gold. It's the last word in luxury.

When finished, the $5 billion Dubailand theme park will be the world's biggest, bigger even than Manhattan. There's the world's biggest mall, commonly called The Mall, soon to be supplanted by an even bigger mall inside the world's upcoming tallest building, the Burj Dubai. The world's largest indoor ski resort will be supplanted by another, which will feature a revolving mountain (great news for all those who see a mountain and think: *Hmm, if only it revolved*).

Not having much real coastline, Dubai has built more: The artificial island shaped like palm fronds, called The Palms, adds another seventy-five miles. Soon to arrive will be an archipelago of three hundred human-made islands, roughly reflecting a map of the world, called The World. This World is a funny old world: Rod Stewart has reportedly already bought up Britain. And there's no Israel.

For many, this energetic display is a demonstration that only when you cut the brake cable does capitalism get really good. "In the next ten years," reckons free-market journal *Liberty,* "Dubai look-a-likes will spring up around the world like variations on a theme . . . it's either imitate Dubai, or become a petting zoo for those who do."

So how does it all happen? Well, through a kind of magic: an ancient form of magic called serfdom. Workers (largely Muslims from the Indian subcontinent) hand over their passports, work twelve-hour days, and live eight to a room, then send home their wages to families they don't see for years at a time. Work is supposed to stop whenever temperatures top 100°F, which they do often, but that never seems to happen. This is because of one of the truly magical aspects of the Magic Kingdom: Whenever it exceeds 100°, there is officially "no temperature," so work continues. "Hot, you say? I grant you, it might *feel* hot. But to be off the scale would require a scale to be off. And today, there is simply no temperature, scaldingly hot or otherwise. Even though we are, as you say, sweating like a pair of bastards."

But look, they're happy! Oh no, sorry, they're not. Like slaves throughout the ages, the construction workers in Dubai are often very unhappy. Puzzled by a recent wave of strikes, interior ministry official Lieutenant Colonel Rashid Bakhit Al Jumairi declared: "The workers are demanding overtime pay, better medical care, and humane treatment from their foremen . . . But they agreed to their employment conditions when they signed."

Poor workers enslaved by the forces of kitsch: It's very much the future! "Can I have my passport back so I can see my family again?"

"No! You must finish building this water park made from gold . . ."

Of late, there has been a spate of workers committing suicide by walking into traffic. (If their deaths are deemed to be accidents, their families back home receive their pay packets.) In Dubai, even suicide isn't really suicide. That's postmodernism for you, to match the sixty-floor apartment blocks in the shape of Big Ben, the Eiffel Tower, and the Leaning Tower of Pisa.

DVDS WITH ADS YOU CAN'T SKIP

The target group for these ads is quite small—the sort of person who wants to watch the same *40-Year-Old Virgin* clip *every single time they use their DVD.* Because certain studios have ensured that the option of skipping the ad reel and going straight to the menu has been disabled. Ho, ho, ho, there's Steve Carrel awkwardly describing boobs. Again.

The other thing DVD production bastards do is stop you from skipping the copyright information—and then put it in 782 different languages, with a running time of seven hours. Just in case you thought it was perfectly legal to burn copies of DVDs but only if you went to Norway and did it.

Non-skippable ads are like Time Warner Cable modifying your television so that if you press the MUTE button during the ads and try to get up for a snack, you get a huge surge of electricity through your sex parts. And even Time Warner hasn't sunk that low. Yet.

E

EARLY IN/LATE HOME

Wrong way 'round.

8TH HABIT, THE

Seven habits must surely be enough, even for the highly effective. Certainly they were highly effective enough to make author Stephen Covey a highly effective billionaire with many highly effective dollars.

But following the initial 1989 list in *The 7 Habits of Highly Effective People,* he discovered another one. And so, in 2004, he published *The 8th Habit: From Effectiveness to Greatness.* This doesn't inspire confidence. Say you wanted to become highly effective yourself, how could you be sure they won't find a ninth habit, or maybe even a tenth?

We're not even up to speed with the first seven habits of highly effective people (although we imagine it's things like getting up early and never finding yourself on a Tuesday evening at last call with someone saying, "Let's go on somewhere else"). But start adding further habits, and very soon you are verily swimming in "habits."

And now we've crossed the Rubicon, where will it stop? This adding of habits could become habit forming. He might start introducing, say, complicated ways to cook fish.

E-MAIL BRAGGING

People who complain about how many messages they get sent, especially after they get back from vacation—"I'm still plowing through them!" Yes, well done. You're really fucking important.

EMERGEN-C

Of all the cold-and-flu-relief citrus-flavored powdered drinks, only Emergen-C encourages you to, quote, "Feel the good." Apparently the more direct "Feel the chalky water" didn't test as well.

Emergen-C is scientific. Science with a capital "Science." Even the tropical ones. The heavyweight nature of this best-selling concoction is reflected in its Web site, encouraging an entire "the good" lifestyle with links like "share the good," "good ads," "good stories," and "worship the good." Apparently if you fight colds with anything else, you're living "the bad."

Oh, hang on, it's just some crushed-up vitamins that tastes a bit lemony. It perks you up slightly, but then so does Gatorade.

What you need to make your own Emergen-C:

- Water.
- Alka-Seltzer.
- Vitamin C. Important note: Make sure the C is capital. Vitamin c will only produce Emergen-c.

ENERGY DRINKS

These days, being given "wings" is not enough. Today's young folk sleep around 20% less than their parents' generation, while being 64% more badass, which means they need 750% more tartrazine, sugar, caffeine, and lurid food dye.

Rockstar energy drink—"Party Like a Rockstar"—plays on rock stars' legendary love of energy drinks. Sometimes they party on energy drinks to the point where they choke on their own energy drink vomit.

Another group with much activity to cram into their busy days are pimps. Their favored energy drink is Pimp Juice, which does not contain juice. They also probably take cocaine.

Or at least "Cocaine," the energy drink with "three times as much caffeine" as Red Bull that was pulled from shelves in May 2007 after the FDA decided the beverage's manufacturer was "illegally marketing their drink as an alternative to street drugs." Don't panic, though: One month later, Redux Beverages began redistributing the drink under the new labeling of "No Name." Because who can focus their eyes to read when they're jittering so much they look like bobbleheads.

ENTOURAGES

Imagine, if you can, being a member of Donatella Versace's entourage. Is it the height of *sophis de sophis*? Or do you fear the night, the dark, hollow times when you believe that you do not even exist?

As we all know by now, from the VH1 documentaries, from the HBO series, or just from the ether, entourages are great fun. Diddy has a permanent video diarist and on-call writer for off-the-cuff speechifying. Mariah needs people to hold her cups, to waft cigarette smoke away from her environment, and also to waft the air when she farts. Shania apparently goes around with grooms for her horses and two sniffer dogs (plus handlers) who sweep concert halls for explosives. (Who could be bothered to blow up Shania Twain? Who?)

Then we can drool over the fabulous gunplay between rival rap packs who, with ineffable willingness, shoot each other's legs off for their main man. Like the incident resulting from 50 Cent deciding to kick The Game out of his own G-Unit entourage. When you're out of an entourage, you're out: not a bit in and a bit out. Out. So outside Hot 97 in New York, a member of The Game's entourage—he, of course, had his own entourage by this point—was shot three times in a confrontation with 50 Cent's new entourage. Another of 50's crew got really confused and sadly shot his own arms off.

All this is clearly guns-a-totin' fun, but all these Western pretenders have so much to learn. They have nothing—*nothing*—on North Korean player-dictator Kim Jong Il. That guy is so boss! Since his debutante days under his father's rule in the 1970s, he's accumulated a truly world-beating entourage, including a multinational team of personal chefs. While "his people" starved—North Korea endured a famine—he imported ovens and two Milanese cooks to prepare his favorite dish: pizza. Extra capers? You bet. "What do you mean, only one visit to the salad cart? With these words, my friend, *you will die.*"

In 1978, when he decided he wanted to build a native film industry, he simply kidnapped the South Korean film director Shin Sang-ok and his actress wife Choe Eun-hee. Kim forced the director to make twenty propaganda films, and sent him to prison for reeducation classes when he tried to escape.

We can but hope that, in years to come, capricious, famine-ignoring, velour-tracksuit-wearing dictatorial kook Kim Jong Il might decide that he needs his own velour-tracksuit-wearing hip-hop/fashion mogul and spirit away Diddy. Maybe Donatella, too. And Mariah. For them, what's the difference? This is the promised land of lifts in your shoes, and a penchant for foreign liquor.

ESTATE AGENTS SHOWING PEOPLE AROUND HOUSES ON TV

ESTATE AGENT: So, here's the bathroom.
PERSON ON TV: Okay . . .
ESTATE AGENT: And, uh, the second bedroom—quite a nice size . . .
PERSON ON TV: Mmm.

It's amazing how often you can see estate agents showing people around houses on TV.

ETHICAL CONSUMER SCAMS

Spotting liberal soft touches from a distance of forty miles, supermarkets have been known to mark up fair-trade goods to make them more profitable than non-fair-trade items. So the small coffee producer is getting slightly more for his goods. The conscience-driven consumer, on the other hand, is getting fleeced to fuckery. This is "ethical," apparently.

Even if you don't buy your Nestlé in a supermarket, world capitalism is not exactly quaking in its Jimmy Choo boots.

Clearly a few small producers getting more for their coffee beans is not a bad thing, but fair trade accounts for only 0.001% of world trade. Even in areas where fair trade is strongest, their market share is puny: 3% of the UK coffee market and 4% of the banana market.

Meaning that, as a strategy for changing the world and challenging the structures of global power, "buying coffee" is possibly not the most effective.

So . . . thank fuck we've got those wristbands as well.

ETHICAL LIVING

Throughout our history, we have wrestled with the complex webs of emotions and reason and social relations and aspirations and power and freedom that define us. Thinkers and activists alike have debated who we are, what we are, and how we should be—from Aristotle's belief that virtuous behavior is inherent to us and would see us flourish as ideal, happy human beings; to Kant's assertions that we should obey immutable moral rules—categorical imperatives to be good; to Marx's ideas that we can't understand humans without considering their social context—that for humans to flourish as Aristotle had foreseen, there can be no slaves, no aristocratic society like Aristotle's, no classes. Plato, Ayer, Nietzsche. Liberals, Christians, Muslims, Marxists, James Lovelock—all of them addressing two questions: *How should I live, what actions ought I to perform?* and *What sort of person should I be?* In essence: Can I be good? How should I be moral? What is right?

And all of them could not see the truths that were staring them in the face and which now we hold to be self-evident. What sort of actions ought I to perform? Buying fair-trade coffee, hemp Frisbees, and a GIVE PEAS A CHANCE organic baby onesie. What sort of person should I be? Smug.

The salvation of humanity lies through the judicious purchase of ethical goods. You can read up on all the new products in special magazines while you fire one out on your compost toilet. You can even buy stuff you don't want or need—it all helps. Let us now take a moment for reflection and self-congratulation by cracking open some fair-trade Sauvignon Blanc.

"EVERYONE'S DOING IT—EXCEPT YOU!" CULTURE

The school playground has long revolved around the question: *Have you done it yet?* By adulthood, the answer is generally yes, so magazines have to invent new questions by changing the *it* from "had sex" to "had sex with three or more tranny geishas in a hot tub?" If the answer is no, you're pretty much still a virgin.

Basically, it's time to get it on with the new sex rules. (What do you mean, you don't find rules sexy?) Women's magazines like *Cosmopolitan* open up this awesome new bedquake by offering cover lines about "Kinky Survey Results" revealing "The Daring New Sex Everyone Else Is Having! Lose your morals on p. 94 now." Everyone, that is, except you.

To prove they have what it takes, too, men's magazines send reporters into the underbelly of this new sexy sex-beast. *Maxim* offered "Dominatrix Detection" or, rather, ten signs that your co-worker might be Mistress Riding Crop. Among the clues: "She's always wearing at least one piece of clothing made from patent leather."

Now, whatever anyone wishes to do sexually, we personally couldn't give a flying fuck (hey, you could even have a flying fuck). But we do wonder if everyone is constantly pushing the boundaries in the same way as the reader of the UK's *New Woman* magazine who, when responding to the Kinky Sex Survey, revealed her "hottest sex ever" was—no lie—"being spanked by a dwarf while tied up." Come on! Everyone else is being spanked by a dwarf while tied up! What? You haven't tried that yet? We thought everyone had done it by now. Oh well.

We've no idea why she was showing off anyway. Spanking is not where it's at with dwarf sex this week. She hadn't even watched a leather-clad Russian oligarch felch a blind Asian crack dwarf while herself manually pleasuring a Shetland pony. Everyone's done that.

EXERCISE VIDEOS

Here is a fun quiz. Which is the weirdest exercise video of them all? Is it:

- *Anna Kournikova—Basic Elements.* Combines a workout with an elementary chemistry lesson.
- *Carmen Electra's Fit to Strip.* Which shows you how to get fit by rubbing yourself on businessmen's crotches and getting implants. Possibly.
- *The Bollywood Dance Workout with Hemalayaa.* Like all things Bollywood, you'll get bored and turn it off after five minutes, yet still tell friends it was totally entertaining.
- *Girls Next Door Workout.* Starring three busty blondes who live at the Playboy Mansion. Watch as they take turns bench-pressing Hef.

- *Tantra Tai Chi for Couples (Adult Educational).* Eh? Eh? We'll say.
- *Denise Austin: Boot Camp—Total Body Blast.* In which the 1980s fitness guru takes on the seemingly unbeatable Russian monster Drago to avenge the death of her friend Apollo Creed. Actually, no, now we come to think about it, that's *Rocky IV.*

F

FAITH SCHOOLS

God helps you learn stuff. Everyone knows this. If God's there glaring over your shoulder, it really focuses the mind on understanding how glaciation works. No one can put the fear of God into you like God. Don't think He can't see you drawing a penis onto Henry VIII's forehead in that textbook. He's a big fucker, too, so watch out.

In twenty-first-century America—a place where people think more about Ron Jeremy than about God—a tenth of all schools are now allied to a faith. The nation is blessed with Catholic schools, Muslim schools, Jewish schools, evangelical schools, Seventh-Day Adventist schools; in Hartford there are even plans for a school that worships Thor, the Norse God of Thunder, where pupils can specialize in bolt throwing, beard maintenance, warmongering, and, of course, thunder.

Now, if people want to spend a year's salary to send their kids to a school without certified teachers just because it teaches that dinosaur bones were buried in the ground by Satan to test our faith, that's their choice. Their stupid, stupid, stupid choice. At least this helps relieve overcrowding in the goat-sacrificing, God-raping public schools.

The problem only kicks in every time the government attempts to redirect taxpayer money into these private institutions, through scams like "faith-based initiatives" or school voucher programs. Listen, conservative America, let's make a deal: We stop bugging you about the right to bear arms, and you stop trying to eradicate the separation of church and state. Cool?

Things are already worse in the UK, where a quarter of all schools are religious, and Britain's most worrying new educationalist is evangelical secondhand car magnate Sir Peter Vardy. At his flagship Emmanuel College in Gateshead, pupils have to carry not one but two Bibles, which, even if you're quite big on the whole Bible thing, does seem excessive.

So how does God influence the teaching? This was spelled out in a controversial document—now removed from the Web site—called "Christianity and the Curriculum," which reckons science classes should show how "the study of science is not an end in itself but a glimpse into the rational and powerful hand of the Almighty." Art classes should show how art can "serve the glory of God and celebrate the complex beauty of His creation." At which point, even the late Bob Ross who painted all those pretty little trees on PBS would start feeling his intelligence being insulted.

The document went on to say—and this is not made up—that history lessons could usefully consider whether, during World War II, Britain was saved from Hitler by God intervening to halt the Nazis at the channel. Meaning that maybe the Battle of Britain film classic *Reach for the Skies* could more accurately have been called *Reach from the Skies with a Big Middle Finger Saying, NOT SO FAST, MR. HITLER!*

We personally think it's a crying shame that no school in the land teaches our own theory of creation: that this whole grand enterprise is merely an imaginative figment of Uncle Mick who smokes a pipe and seems to live entirely on toasted sandwiches. We firmly believe that he dreamed the whole thing up one afternoon while watching bowling, which he loves, and the moment he gets bored, that's it, we're all toast, just like one of Uncle Mick's delicious sandwiches.

We were going to set a school up, but we couldn't be bothered.

FASHION JOURNALISM

Words to go with pictures of people wearing clothes written by girls with misspelled first names (so many z's) and double-barreled second ones.

At heart, fashion journalism isn't about clothes; it's about being so Now that by the time you've finished typing the word *Now* it's too late, because by now you're Then.

Among fashion journalism's key linguistic traits are:

- Sentences that resemble complicated Google searches: "the Kate Moss/Sienna Miller/Mischa Barton school of Gramercy Park bling-meets-boho laid-back high-chic." Keep up, ugly losers.
- Casually dropped French terminology—*au courant, de la saison*—in the style of a yet-to-be-created Mike Myers character.
- Weird boasts. Like "I'm a fashion innovator," "I take classic Armani pieces and wear them in a modern way," "I'm an accessories freak." These are good things, presumably?

- Hyperbole. "Oh Jesus, bite me on the ass these bags of the season are making me so high, they must be a gift from God!"
- Referring to people you have never met by their first names: Kimora, Michael, Lemmy.
- Deification of models. Not just models modeling, but interviews with models about modeling, too! Here's Karolina Kurkova, a model, on what it's like to be a model: "It's not just about being cute. It's about creating something through light and clothes and expressions. It's like theater." This woman was the highest-paid model in 2003, but we should feel very sorry for her: "Modeling looks glamorous from the outside, but sometimes I have moments when I cry." Yes, us too.

Sometimes fashion journalists get paid to write novels, like Plum Sykes's excruciating *Bergdorf Blondes,* a book that has apparently become "a Bible for the fabulously wealthy, the inner circle elite." And which proves, decisively, that you should never read books by anyone named after a fruit.

FAST-FOOD CHAINS MARKETING THEMSELVES AS "HEALTHY" (AND FEMINIST)

"Hi—we're McDonald's, a great big company that would love to come by your house and tell you about how we're changing."

In the 1950s, French artist Yves Klein invented his own color, International Klein Blue, which he believed represented *Le Vide* (the void)—not a vacuum or terrifying darkness, but a void that invokes positive sensations of openness and liberty, a feeling of profound fulfillment beyond the everyday and material. Standing before Klein's huge canvases of solid blue, many report being enveloped by serene, trance-like feelings.

We feel something very similar looking at the pictures of salads in the window of KFC. Or that surreal meal deal with the plastic bowl of rice. You wouldn't actually order these items, but their very existence expresses that corporation's painful identity crisis when faced with a shrinking market. Mmmm. Lovely.

We get similar buoyant sensations by reading the McDonald's Corporation's pamphlet *(We Thought We'd Come to You for a) Change,* posted through mailboxes across the land, which bravely reconfigures McDonald's as a health-food restaurant and general harbinger of world peace. The tone of a spurned lover who treated you wrong and now sees the error of his ways pervades the whole document: "Hi—we're McDonald's," it begins, "a great big company that would love to come by your house and tell you about how we're changing. But there are a lot of us and it takes ages to get organized." That's a joke (no, really) to show us they have a Good Sense of Humor.

"We've knocked the booze on the head and gotten a job. We've moved out of our mom's basement and gotten an apartment: It's not much, but it's a home. It could be *our* home." (We made that last bit up.)

The pamphlet desperately bids to woo everyone back to their formerly favorite restaurant: There are pictures of cute black children, pictures of cute moo cows, parents lovingly clasping their children's hands, and a cute child on a swing—all brimming with salad-derived vitamins. In keeping with the identity crisis theme, there's also a picture of some paunchy dudes watching football in a bar to reassuringly convey the message: Yes, we do still sell shitty burgers that chew your guts up something rotten.

Another section, which contains some of the most remarkable prose ever written, aims to reposition McDonald's at the head of the feminist market (this is not made up). Headlined "You Go Girls," the empowering passage claims that "spending time away from the boys is a rare and precious thing. Make the most of it while you can. Take a shopping break, put the bags down and find somewhere fun to eat." Because, this says, being a carer to men and shopaholic (which, of course, is the very essence of womanhood) is hard work. But where could you possibly have this break? "Yoohoo!—we're over here." Ah yes, McDonald's.

The text—and if you don't believe this actually happened, you can check it out: We've donated a copy to the public library—ends like this: "Girls, before you know it, you'll be back home and showing the things you bought to the boys, and unless it's got cars or football on it—they won't care. So have a great day, have a great salad, and sisters? Do it for yourselves."

FAUX SWEARING

Strolling past The Shop Formerly Known as French Connection, have you ever been driven to splutter, giggle, tap your companion's shoulder, and exclaim, "Look, look—it almost says *fuck*!"? I'm guessing you haven't.

There is nothing big or clever about pretending to swear. If you want to be big and clever, you need to call your shop Ass-Fucking Tit-Monkey's Splooging Cockarama and Co. Now *that's* swearing.

FAX CHARGES

In the Easiest Living Ever stakes, charging people for sending faxes has narrowly squeaked into second place behind being Stedman Graham, who has topped the poll every year since the late 1980s when he first went on a date with Oprah.

At a dollar for the first sheet, followed by 50 cents for each subsequent sheet, a six-page fax sets you back $3.50. With the phone call to send the fax costing about 5 cents, that's a markup of 7,000%.

Your local copy shop or "fax center" Nazi would say that it's not just the cost of the call; they also need the "infrastructure"—that "infrastructure" being a very shitty fax machine purchased in 1987.

50 CENT

In April 2005, Reebok launched a TV ad campaign showing 50 Cent sitting on a box in a burned-out warehouse, snarling at the camera and counting to nine while the screen turns slowly red and a crackly newscaster reminds us how "he's been shot nine times." Oddly, some thought the ad made getting shot look cooler than it often turns out to be.

It's certainly not his clever rhyme skills, so the fact that 50 Cent is now among the world's biggest entertainment figures apparently derives almost entirely from having gotten himself shot up nine whole times—something he doesn't like to talk about. Oh no, sorry. We were getting mixed up with the singer from Hoobastank. In fact 50 Cent loves talking about shooting and getting shot up; he's regularly pictured wearing body armor, pointing massive guns at the camera lens wearing an expression saying *I'm gonna shoot you up.* He called one album

The Massacre; he's always starting beefs with other rappers about who is best at shooting and getting shot up. And so on.

All his bullet wounds were actually attained in one incident, but his image rather portrays someone who has trouble visiting the local bodega without getting himself shot up: "Honey! I got shot up again . . . Oooweee, this one stings . . . got any Band-Aids left or did we run out after last week? Yowza!"

Reebok responded to the complaints by claiming the 50 Cent ad campaign was a "positive and empowering celebration of his right of freedom of self-expression." And not his "right of freedom" to get shot up.

Of course, this is all null and void now that Kanye West beat Fiddy in first-week album sales. Before both stars' new releases "dropped," Mr. Cent swore that if his *Curtis* CD didn't outsell Mr. West's *Graduation,* he would never record another solo CD ever again. Shucks. Gone so soon. At least you'll always have your gunshot wounds.

FILM STARS

Hollywood film stars on talk shows: You have to ask—would you let them near small children?

Here's Tom Cruise (see *Tom Cruise*): laughing much too hard, slapping his thighs, and hooting at stuff that's not particularly funny. Who actually slaps their thighs when they hear something funny? Christ, now he's rocking backward and forward . . .

Oh, and here's Kevin Spacey: talking and moving as though he's been glazed, clearly having given the producers the brief that he will only appear as long as he can try to kill the audience to death by boring on about Bobby Darin instead of tackling any amusing anecdotes about his private life and pets.

Oh fuck, here comes Paris Hilton for her brave, tear-filled performance on Letterman: Actually, Paris's decision to appear on a chat show and not chat was at least fairly radical. She did depart from the whole everyone's-loving-one-another's-company form and become a whiny, crying victim instead. So well done, Paris. You big freak.

FILM WARNINGS

What's a childhood without a few sleepless nights spent haunted by the memory of a grim celluloid bloodbath? Kids love it. Waking up in the middle of the night, sweating, feverishly recalling a zombie slasher hacking at some poor bastard's innards? That's the magic of childhood! Sadly, however, some people don't see it that way and want to deny any potential for trauma with film warnings that seem to get more convoluted by the month.

But really, what kind of person would want to stop anyone from seeing a film that "contains mild peril"? There are, according to some estimates, only seven basic story lines in all human art, all of which contain at least some peril. It's what makes them stories.

And even "mild peril" sounds fairly pathetic, like "mild action violence" or "mild sensuality." If a film is going to include peril, action violence, and sensuality—and, clearly, it should—then ideally the usage should not be mild. At the very least, it should be "moderate."

Who demanded such stultifying detail? There surely don't exist people who read the movie listings and think, *Oh dear God, no! We can't go and see the new Spiderman film, it's got one use of strong language and mild sensuality—if little Daisy sees that, she might die.* Or is this, perhaps, our nation's family-centric right extending its icy influence over the listings in your local paper? Hell's teeth, it's even got "thematic elements"!

To be truly sensitive to a young person's individual fears, we should probably detail everything that may cause offense: "One scene takes place in a kitchen, which features a major heat source . . . plus there is one use of a staircase—down which someone might potentially fall. Also involves moderate use of hair and teeth."

FILMING CONCERTS ON PHONES

You are at the concert. You don't need to film it. You can *download clips live right now*—with your eyes and your ears. It is literally right in front of you. They really should put up some signs: NO PHONE-CAMERA JACK-OFFS! NO! NO! NO! AND ALWAYS! NO!

FISH SYMBOLS ON CARS

Early Christians used a fish symbol to identify fellow believers during times of persecution. These days, to let people know they are really into Jesus, many Christians stick a fish sign on the back of their car. Like BABY ON BOARD stickers—but with God.

Apparently, these symbols have caused belief-system-related mayhem. This is because the symbols don't just mean "I'm the nice sort of Christian who sometimes distributes hot soup to the homeless," but are more likely to mean: "Science is witchcraft and you're all going to hell." To underline the hard-right/anti-science/anti-abortion intent, some fish contain the word BUSH inside, indicating that George W. is "doing God's work."

Incensed, humanists created their own bumper fish symbols with the word DARWIN inside hoping to irritate the Christian right. It worked. They didn't like it. It got nasty. Chris Gilman, the Hollywood special-effects whiz who apparently invented the Darwin fish, said: "Here's a religion about forgiveness, peace, and love, but I can't tell you how many times I've heard about Darwin fish being torn off of cars and broken."

The Christians retaliated with a bumper sticker depicting the Darwin fish being swallowed by a larger JESUS or TRUTH fish.

The humanists shot back with a reversed version of the sticker.

Then the Ring of Fire Web site produced a sticker depicting the Darwin fish and the Jesus fish forming "what Shakespeare jauntily termed the beast with two backs" (they were at it like bunnies).

Nothing will wind up a right-wing Christian more than piscine-penetration faith denigration. And so it proved, with yet more parking-lot/highway altercations. Actually, this is possibly a good way finally to settle the evolution/creation debate: a demolition derby on the highway with the losers ending up bleeding in a ditch with bits of car stuck in them.

If the Christians won, they could shout back at the twisted wreckage: "What's that you said about survival of the fittest? *I can't hear you!*"

FOOD COURTS

Dishes from the four corners of the world! Left half eaten, on paper plates, stacked up, on Formica tables.

The food court: the most monstrous part of the already desperate shopping center "experience." It's like a horrible accident at an MSG factory. And always, as well as the usual suspects, there are chains that you never see anywhere outside of food halls. Panda Express. The Great Steak and Potato Company. Quiznos. What is that? Who is this Quizno? What is this for? Who are these people? *What do they want from us?*

FOOT SPAS

At what point did manufacturers decide that people might need something full of hot water to put their feet in that wasn't the bath? Or, if you must, a bowl? It's like using the normal sink to wash your hands but having another, special basin just in case you feel like giving your pits a rinse.

Other useless items filling up people's cupboards include sandwich toasters and bread makers. We've got billions in useless goods under our collective stairs. What amazing fucking idiots we are. Stick 'em all on eBay in one go and we could probably bring down the economy.

Sandwich toasters are foul, satanic tempters. They seem like a great idea right up to the point you produce your first grilled cheese and the cheese is hot enough to kill you and melts a hole in your hand.

Bread makers are just complete and utter bastards. You assemble the eight trillion ingredients and leave it overnight as instructed—to be lulled to sleep by what sounds like someone being beaten senseless by a marine all night long. Look, it was a fucking present, all right, and we smashed it with a hammer and threw it out an upstairs window. We'd advise you to do the same.

FRAUDULENT RACE-AGAINST-TIME DEADLINES ON TV SHOWS

"Hang on, what's the freaking hurry?"

"Erm . . . well. Nothing, really. Just, you know . . . it makes things more tense. And we won't be able to shout things like 'Wow, I can't believe you painted those seven walls and converted that canal into a home for the blind, all in seven minutes—the drinks are on me!' "

"Oh."

FREE-CD GUNK

You know, that sorta-sticky, sorta-not stuff that holds a free CD or DVD into a magazine ad. What is it? Where do they get it from? Is it bat sperm? Is it hellspawn? Is it mined by infants? We know it has the consistency of nose goblins, but what is it?

FREE MAGAZINES

The ones you have to pay for are bad enough. But then there's all the free magazines—on trains and airplanes, in shops, coming through your door, from trade unions, from insurance companies.

Supermarket magazines never say things like "Of course you'll want to get the vegetables for this recipe at the market, where they're much cheaper"; or "If we're honest, most of our competitors have a much better selection of wines than us. We tend to just get the stuff with the biggest markups or see if it's got a pretty label. Sorry about that." That's possibly because they're less about being informative than about trying to sell you their stuff. Hence, we guess, the age-old adage: There's no such thing as a free magazine.

FUNKY, THE WORD, AS APPLIED TO ANYTHING EXCEPT A MUSICAL GENRE

A yuppie being shown around a sleek urban bachelor pad, on spying a particular feature, will say: "Nice, funky. Okay." A stripped-pine bar-club filled to bursting with vacuous douche-bags will call itself The Funky Monkey. A new handbag with a slightly unusual buckle? That's funky. So, too, is a reasonably colorful mug.

So forget any earlier associations (adj. from the French *funquer,* meaning "to give off smoke" through to "being enticingly odorous" and on to "being rhythmically badass"). Now we must presumably imagine James Brown backsliding across some varnished floorboards holding a chrome tea press and going: "Urrgh!" With Funkadelic all sitting on little stools behind the breakfast bar.

And how "funky" is that?

G

GADGET BORES

William Morris said you should have nothing in your home that is not either beautiful or useful. So we wonder what he would make of boring bastards crapping on about their new sat-nav handheld spaz-top.

GADGET BORE: Look, it shows you all the streets and tells you where to turn.

WILLIAM MORRIS: But you've been doing that journey every weekday for four years. You already know the way. Also, this wallpaper's shit.

GADGET BORE: Shows you where the nearest shoe shops are. You know, for if you need, erm, laces. Do you want to see my iPod playlist?

WILLIAM MORRIS: Cobblers to your iPod playlist. That IKEA table? It's bollocks.

If further proof were needed that electronic gizmos are just a way of filling the void, it is that the magazine for gadget bores is called *Stuff.* That's not even a proper name. What are you interested in? Stuff. That's just stupid.

Mecca for gadget bores is Tokyo's Akihabara, or "Electric Town," which the guidebooks describe as a dense maze of neon straight out of *Blade Runner* with electronic widgets so amazing you will probably want to sign up to be turned into an android. However, if you go to Akihabara, you will find it's more like a really, really big branch of Best Buy where everything is in Japanese. The mutating neon may as well carry the slogan NOTHING TO SEE HERE. New mobile phones that aren't out here yet? Guess what: They look just like mobile phones that are out here yet. That is not, at the end of the day, when it comes down to it, very interesting at all.

Later, emerging into a dimly lit side street, you will almost be run over by what looks like a Japanese Nick Cave driving the smallest car you have ever seen.

GEOGRAPHICALLY INACCURATE RACISM

At a middle school somewhere, an Iranian kid is being called "Saddam"—several letters and one very long war away from accuracy.

If people do have to be racist, do they also need to be so droolingly brain-dead that they can't tell which ethnic group they are rabidly insulting? Maybe they should make special racist maps.

GLOBAL WARMING SKEPTICS

If you're worried about global warming, you must be some kind of pussy. The ice caps aren't melting. There aren't more forest fires or old people dying in heat waves. The seas aren't getting substantially warmer—and even if they are, which they aren't, the fish are absolutely loving it!

We know this because of a small cabal of scientists who believe in big business more than life itself and who, funnily enough, often receive funding from Big Oil. These "skeptics" get everywhere: by the president's ear; near big business; on news programs keen to stir up "debate" and show they're not biased against frothing nutjobs.

In 2004, Myron Ebell, a director at the Competitive Enterprise Institute, told the British media that global warming fears were "ridiculous, unrealistic and alarmist" and that European countries were "not out to save the world, but out to get America."

In 2005, White House official—and former oil industry lobbyist—Philip Cooney was found to have filed reports on the link between greenhouse gases and climate change with dozens of amendments that all exaggerated scientific doubts. That was before he left the White House for a job with . . . ExxonMobil! Could you make it up? Probably, but there's no need.

All this despite the fact that virtually all other climatologists—the ones without links to the fossil fuels industry—now predict that even a conservative rise of 2.1 degrees will probably result in tens of millions of people losing their lives. Even a suppressed Pentagon report warned of a danger that far outstripped terrorism, mega-droughts, famine. Thanks to a newly submerged Gulf Stream, by 2020 the British climate could rival Siberia's. Thankfully, President Bush responded immediately. By standing proud alongside the British prime minister and declaring: "We need to know more about it."

More about what? You can see how this thing will develop in years to come . . . But Myron, I've just put a page of

A4 paper in sunlight and watched it spontaneously combust. "Sheer alarmism—we've always had hot days!" But Myron, a herd of gazelles has just elegantly pranced past the window of our Manhattan studio. "Er, yes, they're mine. I brought them along with me. That big one—he's called Dave and he likes nachos."

And Myron, now you're being swept into the skies by a freak tornado. "What a funny thing you are! I see nothing extraordinary in this turn of events . . . It's great up here! Hi, George, good to see you! Pretty breezy, I know! You what? You want to know more about it? It's okay, I'm on it!"

GOOD AND EVIL AS DEMONSTRATED IN THE MARKETING OF AUTOMOTIVE TRANSPORT

Now, more than ever, we need a firm moral compass to guide us through our treacherous age. Let us be thankful, then, for car ads.

It might not have escaped your notice that many of the ads are car ads. And you might well admire the way many cars embody very distinct moral attributes. Some cars are repositories of goodness that make you feel honest, real, and true—like getting emotional about the memory of *Brokeback Mountain* while sitting in a hedge.

Other cars, very different cars, make you feel dark, cruel, and sleazy, like you're eating a dirty burger for breakfast in preparation for a day's gunrunning.

Very much in the former camp, the new Nissan Note understands that having kids is the greatest adventure in the world (it's not, though—skydiving is: it's over quicker, and people don't clam up when you talk about it). Billboards show this vehicle of virtue speeding through the countryside with a kite flying behind in the clear blue skies. It's wholesome, pure, and pure, like Coldplay's Chris Martin, fresh from having a bath, smelling a fragrant meadow at dawn.

Alternatively, if the idea of going on holiday with children makes you feel nauseated, there's the infamous ads for the European Ford SportKa, which gained worldwide notice for showing a sentient hatchback decapitate a cat with its sunroof. Seriously. All to brag that this car is—again, no joke—the "evil" alternative. All that was missing was the tagline: *You'd better be one sick puppy to drive this baby. Ford SportKa.*

Or you might prefer something closer to nature. "Go Beyond," says Land Rover. Appreciate nature, the hills, the beaches, the misty forests . . . by driving through a misty forest, in a Land Rover! Because the Land Rover is the only off-road vehicle that naturally occurs in nature. Land Rovers are actively beneficent—like sharing cherries with an Eskimo would be good. Maybe the Eskimo has never had cherries before, and you'll laugh and laugh and laugh.

Or you might prefer batshit crazy. In which case, enjoy the VW Polo. A controversial viral Internet ad shows a Middle Eastern suicide bomber driving up to a café in the Polo—but when he triggers the bomb, the ensuing explosion is contained within the Polo. Why? Because the Polo is *that tough!* It is the *only* car that can contain terrorism! If you love freedom and dead bad guys, *buy VW!*

So the choice is clear: You can drive a car that's truly at one with the cosmos, that will make you feel like the Buddha on a mellow tip. Or you can drive a car that thirsts for blood. At least until these two eternal opposing forces come crashing together in a final titanic struggle that will see the skies rent asunder, the ground shake, and the seas get decidedly choppy. At this point, the lamb will lie down with the lion. The shepherd will lie down with his flock. It will rain cats and it will also rain dogs. The beetles will lie down with the monkeys. The Green will lie down with the Black. Everyone is lying down. *Brm brm.*

GRAVITY-DEFYING CREAM

Clinique's Anti-Gravity Firming Lift Cream is marketed to women as preventing the inevitable downward effects of the aging process: "A lightweight oil-free formula [that] helps firm up skin instantly and over time [helps] to erase the look of lines as it tightens. Anti-Gravity Firming Lift Lotion by Clinique restores supple cushion to time-thinned skin."

Of course it does.

Things known to science to defy gravity: airplanes, missiles, space rockets. Things known to science to not, generally speaking, defy gravity: magazines, cookies (not even very light wafers), pants, cream.

GRAVY TRAIN, THE

Transport for bastards, laid on by The Man.

Not to be confused with: the gravy boat, which is transport for gravy, by Your Mam; "Love Train," which was laid down by the O'Jays.

GUINNESS BOOK OF WORLD RECORDS, THE

Genuine Guinness world records include making the World's Largest Dog Biscuit or constructing the Fastest Thirty-Level

Jenga Tower. Why not just go for the World's Single Most Pointless Individual Obsessively Engaged in a Heart-Sinkingly Futile Act?

The Guinness world record for holding the most Guinness world records is held by Ashrita Furman of New York—including Longest Milk Bottle Head Balancing Walk. This fucking freak walked eighty miles with a fucking milk bottle on his empty fucking head. Furman also holds the Milk Crate Balancing on Chin record, the Fastest Pogo Stick Jumping Up the CN Tower record, and the Orange Nose Push—Fastest Mile record (24 min. 36 sec. Woo! Woo!). Since the 1970s, he has set more than eighty Guinness world records. As of November 2004, he held twenty: This means that people see these pointless records and then aspire to break them, presumably saying things like, "434 games of hopscotch in a 24-hour period? Ea-sy!"

Ashrita puts his amazing success down to his daily meditation regime. After discovering the spiritual teachings of Sri Chinmoy, he renamed himself Ashrita in 1974. His real name is Keith (you couldn't actually make this up). GuinnessWorld Records.com explains: "Ashrita is on a spiritual mission and uses his inner spirit to perform the record-breaking feats. Under the instruction of his guru he says he's been able to attain a new level of self-transcendence—meaning he can overcome the physical pain and mental anguish of his testing record attempts."

Didn't fancy using your "inner spirit" and "self-transcendence" for, say, the attainment of world peace then, Keith? At least Furman merits inclusion in the book. So many people are setting world records that many don't even get a mention. Imagine that: You've just set the record for the Longest Jack-Off in a

Bath of Beans, and it's not even in the book. How are you going to feel then?

The book—the best-selling copyright title of all time, at more than one hundred million copies (haven't all these people considered going for a walk or something?)—was set up (in the 1950s) and edited by Norris McWhirter (with his brother Ross), who was not far off being a fascist. He was forever funding strike breakers and defending sportspeople who went to South Africa during apartheid. A rabid anti-European, McWhirter was caught altering the 1975 edition book proofs just before they were sent to the printers, adding: "World's Worst Country: the Krauts."

H

HANDBALL

People would take the Olympics a lot more seriously if they didn't include handball. They're just throwing a ball to each other like a bunch of kids. It's just stupid. And if you win, how do you look, say, the marathon gold medalist in the eye?

HANDBALL GOLD MEDALIST: What did you get your gold for?

MARATHON GOLD MEDALIST: I ran twenty-six miles in extreme heat.

HANDBALL GOLD MEDALIST: Great. I threw a ball back and forth for a bit with someone about two feet away from me. Then I had a bath.

MARATHON GOLD MEDALIST: Go die, ass-clown.

HARE KRISHNAS

Hare, hare krishna
Hare hare
Hare bullshit
Bullshit
Bullshit krishna

Hare bullshit
Bullshit hare
(REPEAT)

TERI HATCHER, PHILOSOPHER

As Bertrand Russell once noted: "Philosophy bakes no bread." This is true: Philosophy is no baker. And bread has never been especially beneficial to philosophy. But that all changed when one modern philosopher was struck by inspiration while thinking about bread. Toasted bread. Toast, in fact.

The philosopher in question was, of course, Teri Hatcher, philosopher, whose subsequent treatise *Burnt Toast: And Other Philosophies of Life* expanded upon her belief that, when presented with burnt toast, women often eat it rather than throwing it away and starting again. The thing is, it's not just about toast—the toast is a metaphor, you see. For all poorly prepared breakfasts. Not that Teri Hatcher seems to ever eat breakfast, what with her looking so thin and all. Or, indeed, a PowerBar.

Anyway, what follows is a kind of aphoristic free-for-all reminiscent of the work of Friedrich Nietzsche. For instance: "When my waters broke with Emerson, I was in the middle of cooking dinner. I called the doctor who told me to come straight to the hospital. I asked her if I had time to blow dry my hair. She said, 'What?' "

And: "When I hung up the phone I burst into tears. That motherfucker. I opened myself up and what did I get? Scorched. I rallied a couple of girlfriends for burn-victim treatment."

And: "When we're kids, our instincts are raw and untempered by all the pros and cons and second-guessing that take over our adult lives. But we suffer the consequences. I kept the cat. Kitty was her name."

Fairly soon, you realize that the desperation is no act, that Hatcher really is that desperate—for truth! Among other things.

We wonder what Eva Longoria's great philosophical investigation will reveal. She's certainly due her own "eureka" moment sometime soon. What with all that sitting around in the bath.

"HAVING ONE OF THOSE DAYS?" ADVERTISING

Having one of those days? Someone at the office dumping their work on you? Got rained on at lunch? Hair? Him? And that?

Don't worry, girls. Just relax on a big, snuggly sofa with a steaming mug of hot chocolate (lo-cal, natch!) and think about crummy guys, etc., etc. With ads for products aimed primarily at females aged 20–35, you can virtually hear the brains of lumpen creatives filling in the cliché boxes with a big lazy tick: okay . . . vulnerable, likes snuggling up, "having one of those days?," shake it all off with . . . bubbles, thinking about crummy guys, lo-cal hot chocolate . . . pamper pamper, more hot chocolate, mmmm, steamy and warm, mmmm, bubbles, luxuriant bubble bath absolutely everywhere . . . "having one of those days?" . . . more bubbles. Candles!

HEALTH-FOOD ENTREPRENEURS

Wholemeal breadheads.

HEDGE-FUND BOYS

In a get-rich-quick world, hedge-fund boys get rich the quickest. How they spend their cash influences whole lower stratospheres of vacuous consumption. Currently, hedge-fund boys prefer to splash their cash ordering bottles of every liquor under the sun, ostensibly opening their own lounge-side bar within the bar.

If professional watchers of the super-rich are to be believed, these "lords of havoc" (so dubbed by the UK's *New Statesman*) drive the tastiest motors, eat at the fastest restaurants, swim in the wettest pools, and stalk London and New York like Knights of the Bastard Table. The *Sunday Telegraph* estimated that in 2005, around 200 to 300 UK hedge-fund managers carved up $4.2 billion of pure profit among them. In 2005, according to the U.S. *Institutional Investor* magazine, the top twenty-five hedge-fund managers earned an average of $251 million each. The amount of money the world's hedge funders handle could be as much as $1.5 trillion.

So how do they do it? Well, it's tricky. Even people who understand economics do not understand hedge funds. These secretive, privately owned investment companies are massive—if they were a country, they would be the eighth biggest on the planet. But it would be a country you could not visit or even see: Hedge funds, of which there are reckoned to be eight thousand in the world, mostly based in the United States, "fly under the radar" (CNN) and cannot be regulated—mainly because regulators don't understand what's going on, even though hedge funds may be responsible for over half the daily turnover of shares on the London stock market alone. After looking into the matter, the Financial Services Authority, Britain's regulatory body, said: "Fuck it." It's very much like

Deal or No Deal: People claim to know what's going on, and superficially there would appear to be some logic, but actually they're making it up as they go along.

We've looked into it and have to say it sounds a lot like Internet gambling for the super-rich. Investors must place a minimum of a million dollars into a fund; at enormous risk, the fund managers take these tax-haven stashes and place stakes on anything and everything—FTSE 100 companies, commodities, options, stocks in developing countries, anything that might shoot up in price or can be made to. Often they will take the tax-haven cash and borrow against it—that is, borrowing money in order to gamble it; which is exactly the sort of responsible activity that should remain unregulated. When the hedge funders lose their shirts (one Japanese fund lost $300 million in a week), it's okay because they've got more shirts. But often, other losers—like Colombia or Egypt (both of which saw their stock markets slump after the hedge funders parked their mobile casinos in them)—don't have any more shirts. Which makes riding with hedge funders quite a bare-knuckle ride, with no shirt on.

In 2006, the "hedgehogs" came into the light with Hedgestock, a festival in Britain that mixed bands and utterly incomprehensible business seminars ("Incubator Alligator?—sowing the seeds, but do they stay for a cigarette?"). It even had its own jingle, which sounded like the worst thing ever. To the tune of "Sex Bomb," it went: "Hedgestock, Hedgestock, Groovy Hedgestock, a little bit of business and a whole lot of rock . . ." And you thought Lollapalooza had gone "a bit corporate."

HELPDESKS

After being shunted among four different clueless cretins, after an epoch of holding on at 35 cents a minute, being subjected to what must be the world's only extant Deep Forest CD, your psyche oscillating between impotence and rage, there is a voice, a connection, a lifeline . . .

"Okay, I've found a Web site about it."

So, I'm paying you two kings' ransoms plus a small fortune and a pretty penny to browse around software company Web sites, ambling toward some kind of nonresolution that I could just as easily have been stumbling across myself on the very same software company Web sites if I were not sitting here listening to your insensate minion ooze bewilderment down my fucking telephone.

I DON'T THINK YOU EVEN *WANT* TO HELP.

HIP HOTELS

Hip hotels might have boxy rooms, bad beds, and shrill staff seemingly beamed in from another planet. But there's a great selection of Latin chill CDs.

- At Milan's übertrendy Hive Hotel, beekeeping is the theme. Visitors can join in the beekeeping themselves or just relax, put their feet up, and let the staff take care of the bees.
- At Notting Hill's boutique hotel BOEulk, they've got an eight-year-old girl on a swing. Sometimes she sings "Son of a Preacherman." Sometimes not.
- Every room in West Hollywood's Barker Ranch features a mural of a different member of the Manson family ren-

dered in the blown-up-cartoon style of Roy Lichtenstein. Sheets are flecked with fake blood. To further resemble a cult of homicidal White Power hippies, all staff have tiny swastikas tattooed on to their foreheads (guests can get their own done, too).

- Berlin's superb Hotel Hostel has knocked away the interior walls, so guests effectively sleep in unisex dorms. Around the clock, the kitchen staff offer classic hostel fare like sausage 'n' beans and macaroni 'n' cheese.

The word *hip* is actually believed to derive from the Wolof (the dominant language in Senegal) word *hipi,* meaning "to open one's eyes" or "to be aware." Of course, anyone who truly opens their eyes and becomes aware while staying at a hip hotel might well be moved to declare: "I have just become completely aware that I am being totally fleeced for a poky room, crap service, and decor that's like the imaginings of a pretentious mental case."

HISTORICAL RECONSTRUCTIONS

So you've devoted two years of your life to a prestige documentary series about Auschwitz. You've got hitherto unseen photographs, interviews with survivors, shitloads of CGI, and a narrator with more authority than Charlton Heston. But there's still something missing. What if viewers think you're making it all up? It could happen. You've been reading all about this David Irving guy.

So, obviously, you hire some actors to dress up in German uniforms and stand in a field (possibly in Poland) pointing meaningfully at a map. Ah, so *that's* what Nazis looked like.

Thank God for that. Because I thought they just wore pinafores and hoodies. That silly walk! It's mad!

The makers of the recent documentary *Munich: Mossad's Revenge* had the cunning wheeze of juxtaposing contemporary footage of Palestinian terrorist suspects assassinated by the Israeli secret service with reconstructions featuring actors who looked nothing like them. Unless you were drunk, squinting at them through tracing paper. Which is not something you do often. Anymore.

During one revenge job, future Israeli Prime Minister Ehud Barak was obliged to dress as a woman to get close to his target. To illustrate that this *really happened,* the docudrama makers re-created the event using the world's shittiest transvestite, thus giving the impression that Mossad entrusted the biggest, riskiest operation in its obsessive mission to track down and eliminate its sworn enemies to Dr. Frank-N-Furter.*

HITLER, PEOPLE CALLING EACH OTHER

The Bush administration loves comparing people to Hitler. Iran's president, Mahmoud Ahmadinejad, is apparently considered a "new Hitler." Much-missed Defense Secretary Donald Rumsfeld compared everyone to Hitler. Abu Musab al-Zarqawi in hiding was like "Hitler in his bunker." Saddam Hussein has joined the pantheon of failed, brutal dictators, "alongside Hitler."

---

*We have been asked to make it absolutely clear that, to the best of our knowledge, Dr. Frank-N-Furter has never worked for Mossad—neither as an agent nor as an agent of influence. Although they did attend a midnight screening on at least one occasion, only to run for the exits when rice was thrown at them.

Even Venezuelan "people's hero" Hugo Chavez was like Hitler because "he's a person who was elected legally—just as Adolf Hitler was elected legally." (The presumed implication: Because George Bush was not elected legally in 2000, he is therefore unlike Hitler.)

In retaliation, Chavez compared Bush to . . . can you guess? That's right, to Harold Lloyd: "He's always hanging off clocks, like a goddamn fool." Not really; it was Hitler. And he added: "Mr. Tony Blair is the main ally of Hitler." (So who does that make him: Eva Braun?)

Chavez didn't call hideous Zimbabwean despot Robert Mugabe "Hitler," though. Instead, this ally of workers everywhere said: "He is my friend. Have you met him?" Of his various crimes against humanity? "We all make mistakes." Yes, but ours generally involve losing our keys, and far less slaughtering of the innocents and starving and impoverishing entire populations.

Perhaps feeling slightly left out, Mugabe compared *himself* to Hitler (no, really), only more so: "Hitler tenfold." Because he, too, wanted "justice for his own people." Yes, that was Hitler all right: justice, justice, justice.

Changing tack slightly, Mugabe also compared Bush and Blair to Hitler and Mussolini. But can Blair really be like Mussolini when he has already been compared to Hitler by the countryside marchers? HITLER 1936. BLAIR 2002, claimed one banner. (Hitler famously hated the countryside, too: "Blood and soil? Basically, it smells of shit and I do not like it.")

North Korea called George W. Bush both an "imbecile" and a "tyrant that puts Hitler in the shade." So, he is Hitler, but in a Jim Carrey sort of a way. But not—NOT—as good as Chaplin in *The Great Dictator*.

Noam Chomsky is "the world's leading intellectual." Intellectuals are paid to see things differently, and Chomsky certainly succeeds on this score. His latest work, *Failed States* (yes, he means America), holds that the United States has been whipped into a state of "demonic" scariness to rival National Socialism. Don't forget that "[Goebbels] boasted that 'he would use American advertising methods' to 'sell National Socialism' much as business seeks to sell 'chocolate, toothpaste, and patent medicines.'" He forgets that it was rare for Hitler's popularity ratings to fall to 32% (unlike Bush's). In fact, they usually hovered nearer the 100% mark. Certainly we would have thought it would be intellectual not to play fast and loose with the definition of fascism, but maybe we just don't have the requisite number of degrees in conspiracy theory studies.

Bush and Blair, of course, never compare themselves to Hitler. They prefer comparisons to Winston Churchill, who was on the other side . . . and won. During the Iraq War, Blair apparently had to be restrained from turning his Downing Street office into a replica of Churchill's war bunker in the Second World War (perhaps forcibly, who knows?). "We wouldn't let him," said close political adviser Sally Morgan. "It would have looked awful. He really would have liked a sandpit with tanks." We would like to offer a corrective on this point. Yes, it would have been awful. But it would also have been very, very funny.

And it could have enabled Blair to face down the critics attacking his "bunker mentality" with some of that trademark gall: "I would say to you this: I *do* have a bunker mentality. I'm sitting in a bunker right now. What do you expect? I'm sitting in a bunker."

HOMOPHOBIC CHRISTIANS

Casting around for the one true path in life, Christians often ask themselves: *WWJD?*—"What would Jesus do?" Apparently, He wouldn't "make some stuff out of wood" or "cure the sick," but would walk up and down the high street with a big placard reading GOD HATES FAGS.

The "Jesus as uptight, bigoted sociopath" reading of the Bible is proving incredibly popular with the world's rising band of evangelicals. Even the born-again movement's preeminent marketing arm Alpha USA—home of the meaning-of-life-answering "Alpha course"—has raised hackles after British founder Nicky Gumbel claimed the Bible "makes it clear" that gays and lesbians need to be "healed." "Although I strongly advise you not to say the word 'healed' to them," he once warned. "They hate that word!" Sound advice.

Normal people flicking through the Good Book will find anti-gay sentiments quite tricky to unearth. The New Testament's supposed "No to Homos" message basically boils down to Paul the Apostle's comments in Romans 1:26–27 on the sins of the Gentiles—"God gave them up unto shameful affections"—and depends on the translation of the mysterious ancient Greek word *arsenokoites* (and we promise that's actually true), which might mean "special gay friend" or possibly "male temple prostitute" or even "gigolo for rich women." Now there's a solid bedrock for bigotry if ever we saw one.

For others, though, the Bible is just one big old book about hating queers; they're constantly finding startling new chapters like when Jesus, after healing the sick and helping the poor, draws together His disciples and tells them how God's vision embraces everyone—prostitutes, paupers, lepers, even tree-climbing tax inspectors . . . "On hearing this, His disciples pauseth for a moment and said unto Him, What about the gays, Lord? Jesus flincheth and spat, Oh no, not the gays. I don't like them, He ranteth. I don't like their white vests or their love of gaudy music. And I have it on the highest authority of a man down the tavern that there's a gay mafia running the Roman Empire. A man with another man? No way! Anyway, the lepers . . ."

In fact, the Big Bad Son of God never mentions bum sex or any other gay-related issue even once, not even mutual masturbation. It's possible He planned on making His Big Speech Against the Gays right after Easter. We'll never know.

HORSERACING TIPS

When it boils down, what you're being asked to do here is take financial advice off a gambler. Is that wise? These are people prone to investing large sums of their own money on chance events, and then jumping up and down exhorting horses to "run quicker, you fucking horse, you," so they are not necessarily the model of an independent financial adviser.

Tipsters are obsessed with "value." The first aspect of this is looking for an event priced higher than its actual likelihood. So if you can find a horse priced at 12–1 when really it should be 8–1, bet on it, quick. Never mind if it has much chance of winning—just remember that, if it does, you'll have four times as much money as you should have! Barman—drinks for all my friends. It probably won't win, though.

Of course, the theory is that some value bets come off, so over time a few big winners will cancel out your losses: The odds are greater than the probability, so in theory it has to even itself out in your favor. This may or may not happen, but for it to apply you'd have to bet on every overpriced event, which would certainly keep you busy. And that's what value is all about.

Except it's also about avoiding bad value. What this means is, in a race most likely to be won by one clear favorite—which thus is trading at very low odds—you look for a horse with better odds to bet on: the weight of money being slapped on the big, strong, fast horse that is probably going to win is making the price "too short" to be worthwhile. And the low price of the favorite makes the price of all the other, not-so-fast horses greater. It's an attractive proposition: Your new selection might be trading at, say, 14–1, so you'll win fourteen times as much back. Barman—drinks for all my friends. Except they're advising you to bet on it "just in case" it wins. Which, in all likelihood, it won't. Probably the strong favorite will. Or it might get beaten by a "live one," only not the "live" one you bet on, which turned out to be more asleep than alive for most of the race.

Tipsters will often refer to making a selection for a particular race as "solving the puzzle." But while a puzzle has a fixed end—the picture on the box of a jigsaw puzzle, for instance—the only fixed point in a horse race is the finishing post. Which horse will run past it first, however, is open to quite a few variables. The horse only has to clip a fence, have an off day, or get a bit tired out and your jigsaw puzzle's flying up in the air in as many pieces as your torn-to-shreds and discarded betting slip.

So if it's a puzzle, it's a 4-D puzzle that constantly shape-shifts, the selection of roses becoming a painting of the White House; then one of the pieces falls over and gets shot through the back of the neck inside a little tent.

Of course, the real problem facing tipsters is that they have to make a call for each and every race. In closely fought races, or if they just haven't got much idea who will win, tipsters will use words such as *might* and *could,* as in *could go close.* This is code for: "Well, you never fucking know. The jockey's wearing blue, and that's my lucky color. How many days to the solstice? Fuck."

It would perhaps be better to suggest you stick a pin in the race card, or say: "Don't bet on this race, it's a bitch, bet on another one. If I were you, I'd get some contacts in the trade who are going to run a mustard first-timer at Saratoga Springs. That's what I do, although obviously I'm not sharing that information with you. Not even if you ring my seven-dollars-a-minute premium-rate tips line for the requisite half an hour of waffle before I finally deign to tell you that the hot favorite in the 3:20 at Belmont is probably going to romp it, which you already knew anyway."

"HOT" COLLECTIVE COVER SHOOTS

Whenever magazines or color supplements suffer crises of faith over whether they are still "hot" or, in fact, "not," they usually gather together a stellar array of undeniably hot, sometimes even hotter-than-hot, really actually quite burny-hot young things for a big old cover shoot that will jump off newsstands with an eye-grabbing headline like "New York's Hippest Designers of Hip Stuff," "37 Hottest Writers of Hot Books Under 37," "The Hottest Human Rights Lawyers in Hotsville," or "This Week's Hot Hollywood Hotties—In Their Hotpants!"

Inside, the editor's letter will say: "Can you feel the heat? Hot off the presses, here's the latest hot young things—they're hot like hot cats on a hot tin roof, like inappropriately hot soup on a hot summer's day, like hotcakes, hot tubs, hot potatoes, and those hot towels you get in Chinese restaurants. Hot! If things were any hotter around here . . . oh, hang on . . . I appear to be melting . . . look at that, I'm actually melting! Aaaaargh!"

What everyone in these pictures should realize is that, as soon as the shutter clicks, they will start to cool. By the time they leave the studio, they will already only be "warm." In a year's time, nobody will remember even the slightest thing about them.

HOTDESKS

We can understand why you might want fewer desks than employees—to keep them "motivated," that is, to create some kind of Hobbesian war of all against all, everyone doomed to insecurity and battling for scarce resources, never allowed to settle in one place and get the idea that they may have a job to come to tomorrow rather than being expelled at speed down a garbage chute into a vacuum.

But do you have to make them hot as well? Is insecurity not enough that you have to fucking scald people? Jesus—actually burning your workers; it's positively barbaric.

"HOW I GOT MY BODY BACK"

"I didn't eat anything."

I

IKEA

When IKEA opened its new store in Orlando, security guards were soon swamped by six thousand shoppers grabbing at sofas and shouting "Mine! Mine!" Many collapsed with heat exhaustion, and twenty needed hospital treatment.

Of course, we're not suggesting the company was in any way responsible for the carnage. After all, a visit to IKEA is usually connected in our minds with inner calm, low blood pressure, and a total absence of any thoughts of violence. No, hang on—we were thinking of the park.

IKEA fucks with your head. All you want is some furniture: Why do they want your sanity in return? The layout alone makes you feel like a lab rat. The stores are like psychoactive jigsaw puzzles with moving pieces, designed by a sick Swedish physicist with access to extra dimensions.

They have what look like shortcuts between adjoining sections, allowing you to pop through a little walkway from one part of the store to another. But where you end up won't be where you were trying to get to, even if the store map said it would be. Worse, if you decide you were better off where you were, and pop back through the hole, you won't end up where you started, but in a different section again. Sometimes on a different floor altogether. In a different branch of IKEA.

There are some amazing statistics concerning IKEA. Apparently, 95% of all couples who move in together visit an IKEA within one month of moving in together. Of these, only 3% manage to buy the things they went there for, and 100% of them are related to the staff. Young couples troop into IKEA with high hopes. They emerge as husks. And without having bought any furniture. IKEA still makes huge profits, however—all of which come from those funny Scandinavian hot dogs, meatballs, and cakes they sell at the exit. And from lightbulbs.

100% of people who visit IKEA buy lightbulbs. IKEA does sell very cheap lightbulbs. Everyone buys the lightbulbs because (a) they are so cheap, and (b) they can't come away empty-handed having spent three hours of pain and panic in IKEA.

Everything in IKEA has funny names: You will find cupboards and beds called things like Dave and Philip, or Clare. Or Jurgen-Bergen-Heldenveldenstetser. If you try to buy any of them, you will be directed to a warehouse section where your item—a chair, say—is placed carefully on top of some eighty-foot-high shelves. They will tell you that a man will come and get it down for you. The man will never come.

IMPROVING THE VALUE OF YOUR PROPERTY

Houses aren't for living in, they're for making cash out of. A good kitchen in a $250,000 property can add 10%. The introduction of a classic bathroom, which might cost just $8,000, can instantly add $1 million to the asking price.

But it's easy for beginners to make mistakes, so here we recommend our Twelve Quick Ways Not to Improve the Value of Your Home—which is possibly going to be shown on TV in the new year:

1. Ruthlessly cut out all natural light with ripped-up trash bags over the windows.
2. Scatter pigs' entrails around the landing.
3. Put a big sign on the door saying: JESUS LOVES THIS HOUSE.
4. Shit in the sink.
5. Open up the hallway as a stable.
6. Pretend it's built upon an ancient Native American burial ground.
7. Disappear into the attic. And never come down.
8. In the middle of the living room, build a little wooden town for a fifteen-strong mouse troupe to scurry about in. Call this Mouse Town.
9. Redirect the sewers in any way whatsoever—they're probably not connected in the right way anyway.
10. Take in waifs and strays.
11. Replace your stove with a tiny plastic one made for children that doesn't even have any connections for the gas or electric.
12. Burn the fucker to the ground.

INCONVENIENT TRUTHS

Al Gore's heartwarming global warming documentary *An Inconvenient Truth* is a rotting bag of recycled compost. Okay, it's a film. We are told this talking-the-talk movie has been breaking U.S. box-office records (although it's not clear which ones: possibly those for documentaries made by former vice presidents). Of course, Gore's record on caring about the environment is second to none. It goes right back to the 1980s. (He actually invented it, right before coming up with the Internet and Roller Blading.)

And since his failed presidential bid in 2000, Gore has been campaigning ceaselessly on behalf of the environment, urging everyone to reduce their carbon footprint before it's too late. In fact, there has only been one itsy-bitsy, blink-and-you'd-miss-it, tiny interruption in Big Al's near-lifelong campaign for the environment: the years 1992 to 2000. During this short eight-year period, he was far quieter about the environment. So quiet that even those in the front row of the cinema auditorium, excellently positioned with regard to the surround-sound speakers, would be reduced to lip-reading lips that were not actually moving.

Oddly, this coincides almost exactly—no, completely exactly—with the time he was vice president of the God Bless the United States of A—in the Clinton administration that did slightly less than fuck-all about reducing America's gargantuan carbon footprint.

Shame he took this particular period off from the environmentalism. Because he might have proved quite useful then.

Darn! These inconvenient truths get everywhere, don't they?

INDIE PORNO FILMS

For pseudo-art-house *auteurs,* there is a new game in town: shooting a drearily pretentious film no one would ever want to see if it didn't have someone's real penis being inserted into someone else's real vagina. Pretty soon, Quentin Tarantino will want to get in on the action, so watch out.

The appeal for the directors is obvious: They get to watch people having sex. They even get to order them about in the process. What the actors get out of the experience is less apparent.

Reviled actor-director Vincent Gallo's 2004 flop *Brown Bunny* famously featured a scene in which the actor-director is explicitly fellated by a character played by his ex-girlfriend Chloë Sevigny.

So how exactly did this happen? Maybe he phoned her up and said: "Hi, this is your ex-boyfriend. The one with the cast-iron reputation for asshole-ism. Look, I'm not gonna mess you round, I'm gonna come straight out with it: Basically, it's like this, baby . . . I want you to suck it on camera for this new thing I'm doing. Whaddya mean, is it justified? Woah, yeah! Of course . . . I can't even believe you even asked me that. I'm outraged! I'm Vincent Gallo, important film director! What do you think? That I'd just ask you to suck it for cheap kicks or something? Man, that would be sick! So, anyway . . . that okay with you?"

In which incredibly strange world of strange fucking strange would the answer be "yes"?

INTEL INSIDE TUNE, THE

The four Intel Inside chimes (da-da da-ding!) are played somewhere in the world on average every five minutes.

Intel (da-da da-ding!) commissioned Austrian musician Walter Werzowa (the evil genius behind 1988 yodel-house hit "Bring Me Edelweiss") in 1994 to compose a three-second jingle that "evoked innovation, troubleshooting skills, and the inside of a computer, while also sounding corporate and inviting."

More than a jingle, this is a "sonic logo" that coincides with every mention of Intel (da-da da-ding!). Wait till Intel gets outside. Then we'll be really fucked.

INTERACTIVE MEDIA

Seeing as the TV channels bombard you with a never-ending kaleidoscope of mind-numbing commercials, and thus can by no means be considered broke, why aren't they paying professionals to make their programs rather than asking you to fill in all the time? They are *forever* canvassing your opinion on this, or getting you to speak out about that. E-mail us, they say, press the red button now, text, call in.

Why me? All I'm trying to do is watch the television, an activity I associate mostly with watching and listening and occasionally shouting and swearing and throwing crisps about, not sharing my opinions with an underwhelmed nation. This is the very acme of modern democracy, though: Don't bother going on a demonstration or writing to your senator, just text what's bothering you to *The Situation Room*. Same difference.

The program, by lazily reflecting back to us what we already know, can fill up time without having to go to the terrible trouble of getting people in who might, say, know what they're fucking talking about. Middle East road map irrevocably stalled? Just have a text poll; much easier than finding someone who could, say, identify Israel on a map. Don't worry about informing the viewers, they only want to see Z-list celebs jacking each other off anyway.

And it doesn't matter how many times you and your buddies text during *Best Films Ever,* even if you run up a bill of $9,000: They will fix it and *White Chicks* will *never* win.

INTERNET CAFÉS

Particularly those with threadbare psychedelic carpets, run by a money-grabbing misbegotten who probably owns half of Barbados purely from the profits he makes on printing charges, full of preppy college students doing pretend higher-education courses sending long, banal e-mails home before realizing that there are other preppy college students in the room and sharing their inane platitudes loudly and at length while you are innocently trying to send abusive e-mails to senators using fake Yahoo! accounts and you only went in there because your shitty broadband has screwed up yet again and you have no alternative but to come back here even though the last time you went in they charged you twenty bucks to send a fax and you told the guy behind the counter that you'd never patronize their stinking digital shit-farm ever again.

Some of them are nicer than that, though.

iPOD FASHION

The iPod has been venerated in many extraordinary ways. iPods have inspired songs, athletics, even books, from how-to guides (um, try touching the iPod's only button?) to a treatise titled *The Cult of iPod,* in which author Leander Kahney proclaims, "Fire, the wheel, and the iPod. In the history of invention, gadgets don't come more iconic than Apple's digital music player."

Maybe slightly less extraordinary, but potentially more disturbing in that it's actually real, is iPod fashion. That phrase exists. It is a phrase that exists. The mere phrase *iPod fashion*—which exists—should make you shudder.

There's Karl Lagerfeld's rectangular gilded purse—roughly the size of "a bread bin," oddly enough—which is lined with multicolored cloth and incorporates a pocket for holding up to a dozen iPods. Or some crusty rolls, we suppose. (Incidentally, Karl Lagerfeld now owns seventy iPods . . . the newly thin German freak.)

Gucci recently introduced an iPod Sling, a $200 carrying case with leather trim and silver clasps. Colors include Namba ("shines golden color in direct sunlight"), Chocolate ("rich and dark, almost good enough to eat"), and Deadly Nightshade Returns ("subtle and elegant").

There are even iPod pants—pants with a pocket for your iPod ("Party On with iPod Pants").

There's also a swath of new sleeves and hoods, with one Internet reviewer deciding of the foofpod that "Overall, it's a recommended sleeve for the iPod if you want to get away from the 'skins' scene."

Jesus Christ, there's a "skins" *scene*? We need to lie down.

iPOD POPES

The pope has got an iPod, hip hip hip hooray, the pope has got an iPod and he's coming out to play.

Yes, the pope has got an iPod. Of course he has.

A Vatican spokesperson said: "He is very pleased with the iPod. The Holy Father likes to unwind listening to it and is of the opinion that this sort of technology is the future."

He's up all night, you know, illegally downloading Gregorian chanting.

iPOD WAGES

The iPod city of Longhua has ten factories making iPod components for Apple. Workers can sleep a hundred to a room and earn $27 a month. It would cost them half a year's salary to buy an iPod Nano. Their wages are low even by Chinese standards. At another iPod city outside Shanghai, fifty thousand workers are enclosed in a barbed-wire compound the size of eight football fields.

Yue, a worker in Longhua, said: "We have to work overtime and can only go back to the dorm when our boss gives us permission. After working fifteen hours, we are so tired. It's like being in the army. They make us stand still for hours—if we move we are made to stand still for longer. The boys have to do push-ups."

"And if we make the black ones, we have to listen to the preloaded U2 tunes. It is terrible."

(She didn't say the last bit.)

IRAQ WAR EUPHEMISMS

Having a great big war going on day after day requires a whole raft of new coinages to stop people from getting too hopelessly worked up about bodies falling apart and other things that really shouldn't concern them. The Iraq War has spawned a whole new range of such euphemisms to go alongside old favorites like *friendly fire* and *collateral damage.*

The whole affair was a "preventive" or "preemptive" war—a

safety measure closer to fitting a smoke alarm to protect your home from the danger of fire than to, say, protecting your home from the danger of fire by launching missiles at it. It was also a "war of choice"—as in *car of choice* or *cereal of choice*—which makes the coalition sound like a happy consumer rather than, say, the kind of consumer who bombs shops. *Pacifying Fallujah* became an almost comfortably familiar phrase (like *Educating Rita* or *Chasing Amy*)—with its connotations of a dummy helping soothe a crying baby's distress. During the attack on Fallujah, the Foreign Office claimed displaced residents were "visiting relatives" and the Pentagon labeled the 10,000–15,000 universal soldiers helping interrogate/torture prisoners as "private contractors." Presumably the word *mercenary* sounded a bit, well, mercenary.

U.S. news feeds would talk of another "busy day in Baghdad" before going over to a correspondent who said, "Yes, there's been some developments." On one particular "busy" day, September 22, 2004, the "developments" included two U.S. soldiers being accused of the cold-blooded murder of three Iraqi civilians, the discovery of the beheaded body of British hostage Jack Hensley, multiple car bombings causing eleven civilian deaths, plus a further twenty-two people killed in helicopter raids on Sadr City. So yes, definitely a "busy" day. If you were living in Baghdad, you'd certainly come home saying: "Busy out there today. Busy busy busy! There's what looks very much like a big fucking war going on."

Perhaps next time we could do away with the word *war* altogether and replace it with the words *birthday party*. This will reinforce how coalition troops are calling in by invitation. On entering this "party," we will start dropping "cakes" on the hosts. Unfortunately, this might lead to some "crumbs" falling on to the floor. But don't worry, because we'll wipe up any subsequent mess with "tissues." Lucrative oil and rebuilding contracts will be the "sweets" we take home in our "goody bags."

Despite the invitations stating that the party ends at 4 AM, we might stretch out the fun a little longer, possibly for some years.

J

MICHAEL JACKSON FANS

There was the lady who released doves into the air in response to the liberating verdict, while the man beside her shouted "Praise be!" to the skies.

And the lady who cooked raccoons over a log fire to pass around to her hungry comrades.

The fan who, as every "not guilty" verdict was announced, sawed off one of his own toes to express his gratitude—sadly, but also joyously, running out of toes before the verdicts had ended.

The family from Arkansas who reenacted crucial moments from Jackson's life—the *Motown 25* show, the baby-dangling incident, the Martin Bashir interview, the morphy video for "Black and White."

The SCID-suffering boy in the bubble whose mother was convinced that some tooth enamel from his hero would cure him of his strange, sad condition.

The South Dakotan death cult who all sported white gloves and reinterpreted "Man in the Mirror" in the style of Nine Inch Nails.

The Catholic priest who added a fifth gospel to the New

Testament—"The Gospel According to Michael"—featuring Jesus continually explaining to his disciples that he is "bad, but bad meaning good."

Whenever Michael Jackson fans gather in one place to give thanks and praise, you can guarantee some serious End of Days shit will be going down. Some appeared almost ecstatic that their idol was up for child molestation again. It's nice to have a reason to get dressed up, isn't it? "Hi, sweetie, they're trying to kill Michael again by saying he's into kiddie-fiddling, showing them porn, and getting them drunk and all that kind of crap! Tell work I'm not coming in—it's the End of Days!"

JOURNALISTS WHO NEVER GOT OVER *SEX AND THE CITY*

We were so close. It had been dead for over four years. The images of Kim Cattrall's withered boobs finally ceased haunting our dreams.

Then *Sex and the City* returned—supersized and in movie form!—and with it came an all-new barrage of articles from that certain type of entertainment journalist who never got over the end of the show in the first place. Mostly female, constantly on the search for her own "Big"-type suit guy, these are the only people in the world who still go on "dates."

You're looking for that ideal guy who knows grooming but is also slightly roughed up; whom all the waiters know, who deals stocks and also deals art and respects a woman's independence but will also throw away thousands on an expensive outfit that will make you look and feel fabulous. You do this by filling professionally concerned papers and magazines with articles about how rich people are great and how expensive stuff is the best stuff.

Now, it's hard to say how much the series' portrayal of the New York singles scene is fact or fantasy without doing more research—and that, frankly, is not what this book's about—but if you transplant this vision to the thronging metropolitan centers of, well, anywhere else, you're screwed.

Look: All the money-raking bachelors around most parts are a loudmouthed bunch of dildos who simply want to (a) snort blow, and (b) cum on your face. Sorry about that.

So, while it seems churlish not to wish you luck, please don't get your hopes up. Oh, and if you do ever find your own personal "Big," do you then think you might possibly be able to shut up? That would be just so fabulous!

JUICE DRINK

Juice: It is, almost by definition, a drink. Add the word *drink* to the word *juice* and you might imagine it becomes even more drinky, which is potentially delicious. But no. If anything, it becomes less drinky. And it certainly becomes less juicy. In fact, your average "juice drink" often contains a mere 10% juice; that's compared with the fulsome 100% juice that's always contained in "juice." Which should make people say things like: "What happened there then? What did you do with all the juice?"

What if you needed to unwind after a hard day and dreamed of downing a bottle of tasty wine but the local liquor store only carried something called "wine drink"; then, on returning home, you find the bottle contains just 10% of the wine of a normal bottle of wine (which is 100% wine) while the rest was just spit and rain?

You wouldn't be happy. You might not even get that drunk. And then, when you start shouting about the whole matter outside your local liquor store, banging on the shuttered windows with your bloodied fists screaming "Where is my fucking booze?" you'd definitely have justice on your side.

K

KABBALAH

Back when people imagined The Future at the World's Fair, the twenty-first century was full of jet packs and robots doing your ironing. None of the so-called experts predicted that everyone would be getting into a weird sect vaguely related to an ancient Jewish tradition that sells bits of red string to its followers at $30 a pop. George Jetson? You're a fucking charlatan.

Apparently, the reason that Madonna, Posh, Ashton Kutcher, et al., wear the red string is to protect them against "the evil eye." Seems a strange length to go to stop people from giving you dirty looks, but hey ho. Oh, and it gives you "total fulfillment."

Spreading "total fulfillment" has been the aim of Philip Berg since he gave up his job as an insurance salesman in 1970 to become a bit of a seer. Called the Rav by followers, the American rabbi set up his first Kabbalah Center in Israel in 1971. Clever marketing—and the "donated" labor of followers—has seen that mushroom into forty centers worldwide and a turnover of millions. By setting up both not-for-profit and private Kabbalah enterprises—plus wheezes like the Rav "blessing" businesses in return for a cut of the profits—Berg and his wife, Karen, have managed to build up an enormous property portfolio and although they take no salaries have lavish no-expense-spared lifestyles for themselves and their two sons. The Rav sold a ten-year copyright to his books to the KC for over $2.5 million. That's a lot of red string.

The reason the string is so powerful, says the Rav, is that it has been wrapped seven times around Rachel's tomb on the West Bank. The people who run the tomb claim to have no knowledge of the Kabbalah Center doing this, however, and the Israeli Ministry of Tourism and also for Religious Affairs have stated that no special permits have been given to the Kabbalah Center to enter the heavily militarized area at Rachel's Tomb with large quantities of red string. In fact, the tomb dispenses its own type of red string—although presumably this contains much less enlightenment, what with it being completely free.

The Kabbalah Center is even trying to get a patent on the red string. Presumably this will involve answering the question *How long is a piece of string?*—so at least it'll finally clear up that old chestnut.

Other money spinners include a set of the key Kabbalah texts, the Zohar, priced anywhere from $45 to nearly $400. To achieve enlightenment, you don't even need to read the books—you can pick up their "energy" by just tracing your finger over them. Ah, now I see why it's so attractive to pop stars.

A 1.5-liter bottle of Kabbalah water—which the Kabbalah Center claims is "purest Artesian" water and can cure cancer—will set you back $3.95. A case is $45. In fact, the water comes from a bottling plant in Canada.

Never mind all that, though; what about Madonna? According to a senior figure at the Kabbalah Center in London quoted in the *Evening Standard,* Madonna joined to learn how to control her moods and "how to be more tolerant with her husband."

But we could have sorted that out for her, no $5 million donation required: He's an asshole. It's not actually intolerant to shout at him. We want to shout at him, and we've never met the tool. You fucking live with him, you freak.

KEANE

Keane need to be stopped, immediately, for these reasons:

- Singer Tom Chaplin's face has no edges, like runny cheese.
- Their sappy, mellow piano rock makes you long for the wild, dangerous sounds of . . . Billy Joel. We always promised we'd take a bath with a hair dryer before we'd say those words.
- The title of their debut album *Hopes and Fears* derives from the lyrics of "O Little Town of Bethlehem," which is their favorite when they go carol singing around their hometown of Battle, UK. One hopes a future album is called *Little Donkey (Carry Mary) ('Long the Dusty Road).*
- Look at them! Just look at them!
- Speaking after a 2005 awards show, pianist Tim Rice-Oxley said: "We went to an aftershow party given by our record company. I had a really good conservation with Jake from the Scissor Sisters, who I'd not met before. We did all get pretty pissed, I have to say."

- Singer Tom Chaplin's face has no edges, like runny cheese.
- Understanding the importance of a "consistent anchor," Keane got their own branding consultants—Moving Brands—before signing with their first label, together drawing up a list of buzzwords including *fascinating, innocent,* and *expansive.* When the band signed to Island, they absolutely insisted on retaining control over their branding.
- Singer Tom Chaplin's face has no edges, like runny cheese.
- Chaplin once claimed: "There's always a strong, potent message to a Keane song. Whereas sometimes with Coldplay, you're not really sure what he's on about." Which is only slightly less deluded than if he'd said: "Hello, I'm Iggy Pop. Here's my big willy."
- Just look at them! Again!

KETAMINE

Having a bit of a dance? Don't trip over the a-hole in the k-hole.

ALICIA KEYS

Alicia Keys might well be the greatest soul singer of this or any other age. If the main premise of soul singing was to sound as conceited as possible.

Realizing that what the world needed most was to share her innermost thoughts, this "unbelievably talented" "new Aretha" called her second album *The Diary of Alicia Keys.*

After that, she actually looked into publishing reworked versions of her teenage diaries from the age of nine onward. At the time of writing, she was "just formulating which style I want to write it in: straight based off my life or a little more journal-style in nature."

In the meantime, she unleashed *Tears for Water: Songbook of Poems and Lyrics,* which featured reams of unused lyrics—because, according to her people, there are around a "dozen unreleased [lyrical] gems for every song that makes it onto one of her albums." Her introduction read: "All my life, I've written these words with no thought or intention of sharing them . . ."

Even this was not enough to sate Keys's desire for Keys-related book product. Just try imagining the scene in the publisher's offices when she unleashed her finest idea: a young-adult detective series starring the sixteen-year-old Alicia as a wannabe soul star who betrays a "sometimes dangerous penchant for investigating—and solving—heart-pounding whodunits." For fuck's sake. What does she do? Go into bookshops and note down all the sections that don't have any books about Alicia Keys in?

Of course, it would be quite tragic if, at some point in the near future, the public unanimously decided that Miss Keys was not, after all, "unbelievably talented" but really quite up herself and could, if she really wanted, go and spend the rest of her days in a cupboard. At that point, we would actually pay good money to read her innermost thoughts.

KEYSTONE TERROR INTERROGATORS

The very word *terror* is enough to strike terror into the heart of most people. Personally, we're very much against "terror." We hate it. You could even describe us as being "anti-terror."

But, without wishing to seem needlessly controversial, I do wish the government would stick to doing the "anti-terror" in a way that didn't jettison human rights. Or diminish global standards on what constitutes torture. Or ignore likely big leads. Or ask questions so stupid that they would make a stupid person ask: "What exactly the fuck do you think you are doing?"

Holed up in Guantanamo, Moazzam Begg was questioned about the U.S. sniper John Mohammed (sentenced for shooting eleven people in Washington in 2002), because he was called Mohammed, which is Muslim. He was also shown pictures of the pope taken from his computer's hard drive and questioned about his apparent assassination plans. Begg was initially confused by these pictures, until he remembered that all computers' "Temporary Internet Files" folders store all of the images from any visited Web site. So a visit to the Fox News Web site, say, might lead to your computer storing all sorts of pictures from the home page that you hadn't even paid any attention to at the time. (The interrogators also presented him with a picture of a camel spider and asked him for an explanation, although they did not accuse him of planning to kill it.) The Catholic major told him: "If anything happens to the pope, I swear I'll break every finger in your hands."

On other occasions, Begg was asked to identify someone from a picture of the back of their head, or an arm, or a leg, and asked: "Do you recognize this?" To which he might reasonably have responded: "Hmm . . . tricky one, this . . . [decisively] Singh! Yup, it's Vijay Singh, the golfer . . ." before realizing he wasn't after all on ESPN's *Two-Minute Drill.*

KFC

Why do you never see hippies with scarves covering their mouths catapulting each other through the window of KFC? It's always McDonald's. But Colonel Sanders was a right bastard—just look at what he did to Elvis.

BEN KINGSLEY, SIR

Sir Ben Kingsley has been woefully misunderstood. When he was billed on the posters for *Lucky Number Slevin* as "Sir Ben Kingsley," he was accused of being "barmy" by Lord Puttnam and of talking "pretentious bollocks" by Roger Moore. (*Lucky Number Slevin* wasn't lucky, by the way, it was shit.)

Sir Ben Kingsley shot back, telling the *Sunday Telegraph* that he was "shocked" by the producers' "faux pas." His case was sadly weakened because he was quoted as accepting the knighthood by saying: "There is no Mr. Ben Kingsley anymore. Being a Sir brings with it responsibility." And an old document sent to all crew on his previous movie *Mrs. Harris* read: "We received a call from Ben Kingsley's agent . . . Please address him as 'Sir Ben' if you find yourself in his presence."

It puts one in mind of his most celebrated role, that of Mahatma Gandhi. Except for all the humility, the grace, and the kick-starting of campaigns of civil disobedience. As Gandhi famously said: "I want an M&M-filled trailer the size of Jupiter. Right here. Right. Fucking. *Now!*"

KITSCH KNICKKNACK SHOPS

Called things like Missy Kitty Mau Mau or Puss Puss or Funky Monkey Pants. Sometimes innocent shoppers accidentally enter an emporium because they need to buy a present for someone and it claims to specialize in presents.

Ooh, they think. *A present shop, maybe I can get a present in this shop for presents and thus satisfy my present-buying needs.* Then they go inside and remember that it's actually a festival of shit with price tags on. You can find:

- George Bush fridge magnets—you can dress him up as either Shirley Temple or Wonder Woman.
- A Monkey tape measure.
- Numerous cards featuring the picture of a 1950s housewife and a rude slogan—something like, ON SUNDAYS, DOREEN ENJOYED NOTHING MORE THAN A GOOD SPIT-ROAST.
- A Wonder Woman cocktail shaker.
- A tiny little book about eating chocolate.
- Plastic action figures of a black Jesus arm-wrestling Che Guevara. (See **Che Guevara Merchandise**.)
- A monkey. With the head of Monkey.
- Something featuring a Mexican wrestler.
- A baby's first Ramones T-shirt.
- Monkeys.

Of course, no one really wants this crap. But they get it anyway . . .

EMMA: Here you go, Gran—happy birthday. I got you a T-shirt with PORN STAR printed on it.

GRAN: Oh, cheers. By the way, I never liked you, and your dad's not your real dad.

L

LEFT/LIBERAL APOLOGISTS FOR ISLAMIC FUNDAMENTALISTS

There are some ground rules that need establishing here: blowing oneself up in a shopping center to forward a medieval theocracy involving the suppression of women and the stoning of gays is a bad thing, isn't it? We think we can all agree on that one.

Ah, apparently not. By some crazy twist of logic, reactionary bigots who seek to plunge the world into religious darkness can become freedom fighters—a "deformed" liberation movement; the ACLU by other means. If you don't like U.S. imperialism (and hey, even the Pentagon seems to be wavering on that one these days), you must be okay—even if what you do like is slaughtering people standing at bus stops because of their religion. So we end up with anti-war demonstrations where purportedly socialist paper sellers mingle with thoroughly fundamentalist Hizb ut-Tahrir, chatting, standing next to each other.

There's Rosie O'Donnell, who—when not feuding with other celebrities or acting mentally retarded in the hope of winning an Emmy—fancies herself Long Island's own Noam

Chomsky. Why, during only her second week as co-host of the misogyny-fueling morning show *The View,* Rosie smacked down conservative co-host Elisabeth Hasselbeck's comment that militant Islam is a "grave threat" by stating that "radical Christianity is just as threatening as radical Islam in a country like America." Now, let's be clear: We really don't want to defend Hasselbeck. She's like Ann Coulter as played by Florence Henderson. But Rosie, radical Christianity is many things—hateful, homophobic, predominantly white—but it's not shouting "Death to America" or strapping explosives onto its followers' chests. Not yet. Maybe if Hillary wins in '08 things will take a sharp left turn.

At a later date, Rosie also told *View* viewers, "Don't fear the terrorists. They're mothers and fathers." Um, actually, that makes us fear them more. Terrorist mothers and terrorist fathers mean there are little terrorists running around, playing with "Kill the Infidels" Elmo and whatnot.

Of course, Rosie is but one woman. There's also the mayor of London, Ken Livingstone, who warmly welcomed reactionary bigot Sheikh Yusuf al-Qaradawi to his fair city. (Al-Qaradawi supports the execution of all males who engage in homosexual acts and "personally supports" female circumcision. Of suicide bombers, he says, "For us, Muslim martyrdom is not the end of things but the beginning of the most wonderful of things.")

Historian and novelist Tariq Ali has set himself up as one of the world's premier cheerleaders for the bigots dominating the insurgency in Iraq, casting them as anti-imperialist warriors and saying: "The resistance in Iraq is not, as Israeli and Western propagandists like to argue, a case of Islam gone mad. It is . . . a direct consequence of the occupation."

Critics of this abject moral and intellectual collapse are often accused of "Islamophobia." But this isn't about Islam per se. What we are talking about is Islamic fundamentalism—a fanatical politico-religious ideology that would outlaw homosexuality, kill trade unionists, institute medieval, religious feudalism . . . sort of like fascism, only less modern.

So, all things considered, if ever the worldwide caliphate is established, it seems like a few people will be in for a nasty shock:

THE MEDIEVALISTS: Ah, honored gentlemen. If you'd be so kind as to file into this football stadium . . .

ROSIE: Sure! I love riding buses! Can I see photos of your sons and daughters?

THE MEDIEVALISTS: Yes, later. Now please, hurry it up. We've got a load of stonings still to do—and we'd just like to slaughter you all.

ROSIE: Lovely. I like buses, you know.

TARIQ ALI: What? You're going to what?

HARRY BELAFONTE: They're going to slaughter us. It's nothing to worry about. It's customary among such peoples. Cigar?

TARIQ ALI: Don't they know who I am? You really should have mentioned this before.

THE MEDIEVALISTS: We did.

TARIQ ALI: Oh.

ROSIE: Yes. Now I come to think about it, they did give some signals in this direction. I like buses, you know.

TARIQ ALI: Well, I think it's rude. I'm going to write a big piece in the *Guardian* about it.

THE MEDIEVALISTS: We've burned it down.

TARIQ ALI: The *New York Times*?

THE MEDIEVALISTS: Yeah, that, too. We didn't like the *Sunday Magazine*. Only joking—it was for being infidel.

"LIFESTYLE" MUSIC COMPILATIONS

Like all products with the word *lifestyle* attached to them, these compilations are designed for people who have neither a life nor any style. What they say is: "I do not know anything about music. Please, Clever Marketing People, target my demographic and tell me what you want me to like."

Who thinks these things up, let alone buys them? Take the Elite Modeling Agency Compilation. As the name suggests, Elite would be useful if you needed a model: Perhaps you are a fashion photographer, or have dropped something down the side of the fridge and can't reach it. It knows shit-all about music. Neither do *Elle* magazine or *Cosmopolitan*. *Cosmo* is known mainly for doing questionnaires about blow jobs, which are sometimes related to, but are essentially different from, music.

ESPN's Jock Rock and Jock Jams series of albums are based on a false premise: Jocks do not love music; if they did . . . *they wouldn't be jocks!* Instead of playing football, they would've joined the jazz choir and been beaten up by the football team.

The music label Quango has nonsensically titled compilations available for any ABC drama in need of a musical montage. Dr. Meredith Grey is crying over McHotpants? Cue up the *Mystic Groove* CD!

Describing their extensive compilation series, Starbucks says you should "Think of them as mixed tapes from a friend." We prefer to think of them as mixed tapes from Beelzebub.

LISTS

1. *OK Computer.*
2. *The Bends.*
3. Apple's *1984* Super Bowl Ad.
4. Johnny Carson.
5. Shepherd's pie.
6. Who Shot J. R.?
7. Bobby Ewing in the shower.
8. The sax solo in *Baker Street.*
9. *The Shawshank Redemption.*
10. *The Bends.*
11. *Thriller.*
12. *The Bends.*
13. The video for "Thriller."
14. *The Da Vinci Code.*
15. *Star Wars.*
16. The last episode of *M*A*S*H.*
17. Hank Aaron.
18. The Heidi Game.
19. The Beatles.
20. The otter.
21. Jesus Christ.
22. This certainly is an
23. easy way to
24. fill up the pages
25. and schedules
26. and that.
27. Abraham Lincoln.
28. Lake Titicaca.
29. *The Bends.*
30. *OK Computer.*

31. *The Bends.*
32. *The Bends.*
33. *The Bends!*
34. *OK Computer.*
35. Martin Luther King.
36. The Shining Path.
37. Homer Simpson.
38. *Pet Sounds.*
39. Maya Angelou.
40. *The Bends.*
41. *Godfather 3*
42. was crap.
43. But the first two
44. were not crap.
45. Did you know that?
46. I didn't.
47. Jesus.
48. Jesus Christ.
49. Jesus H.   Christ.
50. Might it just be possible
51. to start producing more culture
52. instead of lazily cataloging
53. stuff that everyone already knows about?
54. Richard Nixon.
55. Lance Armstrong in *Dodgeball.*
56. Help
57. I want to get off
58. but I can't.
59. *The Day the Clown Cried.*
60. Flea.
61. Chuck Norris in *Dodgeball.*

62. No, really.
63. *The Bends.*
64. I'm serious.
65. Nasty Nick.
66. This is killing me.
67. The otter.
68. Super Bowl III.
69. *The Bends.*
70. *Gone with the Wind.*
71. Johnny Carson.
72. Johnny Carson watching *Gone with the Wind.*
73. Might it be possible
74. to just be quiet for a bit?
75. Okay then, let's see about that.
76. Here goes . . .
77. . . .
78. . . .
79. . . .
80. That's better.
81. . . .
82. . . .
83. Pure bliss, actually.
84. . . .
85. . . .
86. . . .
87. . . .
88. No longer . . .
89. hearing the worthless bleatings . . .
90. of a moribund civilization . . .
91. turning everything of worth . . .
92. and integrity . . .

93. into another shitty fucking list . . .
94. . . .
95. . . .
96. *Pulp Fiction.*
97. NO!
98. *Pet Sounds.*
99. NOOO!
100. The "Where's the Beef?" Lady.

LOFT LIVING

In the olden days, factories were for making stuff in. Poo! Smelly! These days, factories have found their proper function: as places for executive dickheads to live in while feeling superior and self-regarding.

Welcome to the "funky" world of "loft living." This is not, as must be made emphatically clear, the same as living in the loft. Executive dickheads do not spend their leisure hours surrounded by Christmas decorations, broken train sets, and fiberglass couches that make your arms itch. No, these lofts are "funky artist spaces." They're "the ultimate in cool contemporary living." Particularly if you have a "cinema kitchen" (and who wouldn't want a "cinema kitchen," if only they could work out what one was?) or a "colorful shower pod."

Loft living began in downtown New York in the 1950s with beatnik artists and writers with absurdly thick-rimmed glasses taking over vast, cheap spaces in disused factories and warehouses south of Houston Street. These pioneering types all decided: "Walls are for squares! I'm gonna spend all day staring at this decomposing apple core from various points around my football-field-size abode."

As the Urban Spaces Web site explains: "The loft offered not so much a style as an attitude. Something that would set you apart from the dull conformity of suburban living . . . The disciplined order of conventional living in specific rooms for each task was about to be eschewed for the romantic notion of the bohemian decadence of open space."

The disciplined order of conventional living in specific rooms for each task? Balls to it. Eventually, of course, all the bohos were driven out by developers. Nowadays, far from being the "cheap alternative to more conventional housing," loft living is actually more expensive per square foot than pretty much any other form of living. Loft spaces now generally attract the kind of person whose primary art involves devaluing random foreign currencies through the medium of computer terminal and telephone line. The kind of person who makes the average attendee at a Nazi rally look fiercely individualistic and bohemian. This is apparently quite "funky."

But that's just the start. With everyone wanting to live in factories, the artists have started moving into art galleries. Meanwhile, all the art is being shunted into bars. Gradually, the drinks-serving aspect of bars will be farmed out to the remaining houses. This will increase the demand for houses—because we all like a drink, however colorful our "shower pod"—and the whole crazy cycle starts again. Factories will start making stuff again, with burly overseers driving the loft dwellers out of their lofts and on to the looms. Southeast Asian economies will nose-dive in the face of sweatshop imports from the United States. America will occupy Mexico, which, after initial resistance, the U.S. populace will support as it brings down the price of salsa, plus everyone's got bars in their houses so they're buzzed all the time and really confused.

And what's "funky" about that, then? Eh?

LOST

Lost interest.

LOW-CARB POTATO

Today we know that carbohydrate is dangerous both morally and spiritually. Previously spuds were cursed with a sizable carb content—they were famous for it. People used to say: "Have some spuds, they're good for you. Spuds are full of carbs—which is a food group."

But now researchers at the University of Florida have developed a new breed with 30% less carbs than the standard baking potato. "When it comes to beautiful potatoes, this one is a real winner!" assured Chad Hutchinson, assistant professor of horticulture at UF's Institute of Food and Agricultural Sciences. He went on to eulogize its light yellow flesh and "smooth, buff-colored skin."

Now, *that's* science.

GEORGE LUCAS

Obsessively secretive movie mogul George Lucas spent years up in his Skywalker Ranch (crazy name, crazy ranch) plotting the second trilogy of *Star Wars* films. The renowned filmmaker, who last made a decent film during the final years of the Carter presidency, would spend hours explaining to his minions how the first *Star Wars* film was actually not the first film but, in fact, simply the fourth episode of a twelve-part saga.

There's a whole new backstory concerning Anakin Skywalker that will show everything we already know in a new light. And there's a Rastafarian frog called Jar Jar Binks. These new films, he would continue, would be far superior to those earlier works because they are "digital." George Lucas loves "digital"—in the late 1970s he was one of the first people ever to buy a digital watch (it could perform Beethoven's *Für Elise,* which used to drive everyone on the *Empire Strikes Back* set absolutely nuts). In the twenty-first century, his prime mission has been to change worldwide cinema technology over from film to digital projection. The new *Star Wars* films, which history would see as his true masterworks, would display the first flowering of this innovation's awesome potential.

At some moments, after spending many hours in front of the bluescreen, one imagines he would become distracted and cackle: "They laughed at *Howard the Duck.* A film about a duck called Howard? Don't be stupid, they said. And . . . well, maybe they were right. But this time! This time I'll show them all. These three films will define the landscape of the blockbuster in the early years of the twenty-first century. At last, Spielberg will be my bitch!

"What's that you say? Someone who actually knows about making half-decent movies is doing *Lord of the Rings*? Yeah, well . . . Those guys haven't reckoned on Jar Jar. Ha! *And* I've got Christopher Lee . . . What? They've got Christopher Lee, too? Oh . . ."

Sadly, George was so distracted by the awesome potential of CGI technology that he turned the most loved film franchise of all time into anus sandwich. This was partly because the CGI-designed Rastafarian frog Jar Jar Binks was seemingly based on 1930s black stereotype Stepin Fetchit. Not only that, but he also based the story on a script so bad that the actors found themselves physically unable to act "excited" or even "remotely unembarrassed" in front of the camera.

Amazingly, Lucas was the only prominent New Hollywood director not on drugs.

M

MAC JUNKIES

"Oh, Macs are just so much better than PCs. The operating system is about twelve times faster and they're just so much more efficient in, ooh . . . so many ways."

Are they? Are they really? And how the fuck would you know, when all you use them for is downloading MP3s and looking at porn? What you actually mean is: "They look nice."

The Mac junkie will also crap on without end about how Microsoft is a big nasty corporation. No shit? And Apple's what, then—a workers' co-op? No, it's a smaller nasty corporation—which uses child labor and beats its workers, whom it pays in beans, with sticks (possibly).

Do you know what Apple employees call company chief Steve Jobs? We'll tell you: Big Jobs. Or Shitty Jobby Job-head. And that's true. Okay, it's not.

MANAGEMENT CONSULTANTS

A flourishing sector of the business world that is employed, at very great expense, by managers in other businesses to explain how to manage—in particular, how best to cut costs.

Remarkably often, consultants' advice comes extremely close to that given by management-consultant-turned-Enron-CEO Jeff Skilling* in 1997: "Depopulate. Get rid of people. They gum up the works."

But—and this is key—*do not* get rid of any management consultants. Or you'll be really fucked.

NELSON MANDELA, PEOPLE COMPARING THEMSELVES TO

In a major interview to coincide with the publication of his autobiography, Bill Clinton revealed that what got him through the Lewinsky scandal and Starr inquiry was the example of Nelson Mandela—who had been in pretty much the same situation.

Clinton said: "[Mandela] told me he forgave his oppressors because if he didn't they would have destroyed him. He said: 'They took the best years of my life. They abused me physically and mentally. They could take everything except my mind and heart. Those things I would have to give away and I decided not to give them away.' And then he said, 'Neither should you.' "

Mandela got into his spot of trouble by fighting one of the most powerful and effective systems of oppression ever conceived, apartheid. Clinton got into his spot of trouble spunking on a young woman's dress.

---

* Currently serving over twenty-four years in prison for fraud and insider trading. When indicted, Skilling petitioned for his trial to be moved away from Houston after a poll showed a third of area residents associated his name with negatives like "pig," "snake," "economic terrorist," and "financial equivalent of an ax murderer." Yes, those are negatives, all right.

Mandela was jailed for twenty-seven years. Clinton was told off a bit.

Martha Stewart, speaking about her impending incarceration for insider dealing in 2004, said: "I could do it. I'm a really good camper. I can sleep on the ground. There's many other good people that have gone to prison. Look at Nelson Mandela."

Stewart's situation would indeed have been identical to Mandela's—if only Mandela had owned a business empire worth $800 million and been jailed for lying to investigators regarding a suspicious stock sale.

Actor Johnny Depp, meanwhile, was so miserable working on the TV detective show *21 Jump Street* between 1987 and 1992 that he tried to get himself fired by pulling stunts such as (and this is true) setting fire to his underwear. Speaking years later about his heroic struggle, Depp said: "I was like Mandela, man."

How true. And what if Depp had not managed to break those manacles of oppression? There would have been no *Finding Neverland.* All together now: "Free-ee Joh-hn-nny Deepp! Free-ee Joh-hn-nny De-epp!"

In the world of international celebrity, you don't need to have been imprisoned to stand comparison to Robben Island's most famous inmate. Or have any discernible beliefs. After all, in his brave fight for what was right, what exactly did Bill Clinton stand for? La la la. Clinton Clinton Clinton—Old Billy Clinton: What did Big Bill C, 42nd President of the US of A, stand for? Nope, nothing coming. Ah yes, that's right: blowing his saxophone, staying in power for a while, having his saxophone blown.

There is, though, one major similarity between Mandela

and Clinton: They are both black. The writer Toni Morrison called Clinton "the first black president of the United States." He wasn't though, he's white—we've seen him on TV. And it's a funny sort of "black president" who, during the 1992 primaries, would fly back to Arkansas, where he was governor, to oversee the execution of brain-damaged black man Ricky Ray Rector simply to look tough on crime.

Maybe Toni Morrison just meant that he was really into hip-hop. Or that he likes saying the words: "You go, girl!"

MARKETS' REACTION, THE

Whenever a new terrorist catastrophe hits a major Western city, the first thought on every citizen's mind is: *Hmm, I wonder how my shares are doing. Oh, that's right, I don't have any. Still, I wonder how other people's shares are doing . . .*

This is why, following the 7/7 London bombings, news networks speedily escorted viewers and listeners away from the sites of the atrocities and toward the City of London to discover how "the markets" might be affected. And what did our market reaction correspondents tell us? Stocks remained "resilient" throughout trading. Thank God.

Showing touching concern for their War on Terror comrades, our own Fox News even discussed how to capitalize on all the murder and maiming. Washington managing editor Brit Hume told host Shepard Smith (great name, Shepard) on air: "Just on a personal basis, when I heard there had been this attack and I saw the futures this morning, which were really in the tank, I thought, *Hmmm, time to buy.* Others may have thought that as well. But you never know about the markets."

Those markets, eh? What are they like!? You just never know.

If we dare tangle with their mysterious workings, they'll be liable to strike down upon us with great vengeance and furious anger. They're like Dennis Hopper meets Krakatoa—on crack! One flick of the tail and, seriously man, we're all goners. If only these terrorists knew what they were messing with . . . well, then they'd be sorry.

To be fair, Hume did get some flak for positing 7/7 as a great day for bargain hunting. But maybe using the instability to make a killing is actually a noble way of doing our duty. After 9/11, one media stock commentator—James B. Stewart of *SmartMoney* magazine—even urged readers to follow his example and buy shares "both as a sound investment and as an act of patriotism."

Momentarily halt the quick-buck roller coaster? You might as well piss on the Stars 'n' Stripes. More weirdly still, some readers responded that Stewart wasn't being sufficiently selfish to be a true American. Surely, he later paraphrased, "Something as abstract and emotional as patriotism was heresy, and that the sole basis should be a rational calculation of economic self-interest. Anything less, they argued, undermined the markets' efficiency and in that sense was actually unpatriotic." To which the only rational response is: "Aarrgh!! Aaargghhh!!" And probably: "Aaaaaaaaaaaaaaargggghhh!!!!"

The message for those with capital to burn is clear: In the event of the next horrific attack on a major Western city, don't flinch from making merry. Don't you dare. To display even a tiny chink of respect or humanity might anger the markets. They'll think we're going pink. Then they'll fuck us. They'll fuck us all to hell. Then we'll really be fucked. Not like we are now. More fucked.

As flies to wanton boys, are we to the markets. (We exaggerate, of course.)

BOB MARLEY MERCH

But Marley is more than just the ultimate signifier of our multicultural world. He is a symbol of resistance. Particularly for middle-class white boys who have always enjoyed pretending to dig him. In the old days, this used to require some effort, such as growing some dreadlocks by not washing your hair. (Admittedly, not washing your hair doesn't require that much effort, but it does indicate a certain stiffness of resolve.)

These days, you can see clean-cut Aryans sitting on trains playing games on their mobile phones wearing Bob Marley T-shirts and toting a Bob Marley bag. Human beings could not physically look less like they were feeling some Rastaman vibrations or were dedicated to the downfall of Babylon.

You look like Zac Efron. You *are* fucking Babylon.

MEDIA STUDIES

After three years studying "the media," I must be a real expert in "the media." Can I have a job in "the media" now, please? Vacuous jerk-offs.

MEN'S MAGAZINE COVER LINES

Pulling in readers (or "readers") to *Maxim, Stuff, FHM,* and other Victoria's-Secret-catalog-with-articles magazines is a fine art. These titles somehow need to convince discerning young men that this month's piss-poor pictures of underdressed women are not exactly identical to last month's. This time, they're so disgustingly enthralling that, on opening the magazine, readers will instantly feel like pigs in shit. So they adopt cover lines like: "Special Report: The Search for America's Hottest Club Girls." (That's real.) And: "Warning: Keep It in Your Pants Till You Get Home—You'll Be Sore Tomorrow!" (That isn't real, but it could be.) Incidentally, if any inspiration-starved editors want to use the line "This Issue Will Make You Issue in a Tissue," they can have it.

Of course, these mags aren't just tits and ass. They also have the trickier job of letting readers "buy into" an inspirational brand that will keep them informed about shaving . . . while still assuring them that there are also juicy pics to rub out onto. This tightrope act is seen when *Maxim* opts for cover lines like: "Sex! Cheating, One-Night Stands, and Your Friend's Hot Sister" or "Office Sex! Naked Ambition Has Its Rewards." Not to mention all their name-dropping like "Hayden Panettiere Loses Her Cheerleader Outfit!" or "Milla Time: Come See the Spread That'd Raise the Dead!" Which conjures up disturbing images of numerous well-groomed young bucks eagerly drooling over photographs of Milla Jovovich wearing slightly fewer clothes while zombies tear apart their flesh.

If you are such a person, you should try using the Internet. Honestly! You won't know what hit you!

MEN'S MAGAZINE PULLQUOTES

The big, bold quotes extracted from interviews with young women to go alongside the pictures in men's magazines are "cleverly formulated," too. The smuttier titles inevitably pick out lines like: "I love my bum—it's great to hold on to" or "Another woman? Sure, why not?!" or "Yes, I definitely think the readers of your magazine would have a chance with me, I really do. I'm sure they're all fantastic lovers."

In the more aspirational titles, when interviewing a bona fide respectable star like, say, Rachel Weisz, the interviewer will awkwardly throw in a quick question about doing nude scenes or having sex. The actress's world-weary, noncommittal answer—something like "Well, okay . . . I guess you could say that I like sex . . ." or "Hmm, my breasts . . . whatever"—will be printed in 40-point bold curlicues to hopefully bolster the impression that she is opening up her darkest desires rather than absentmindedly wondering about lunch.

It will only be a matter of time before these pullquotes are artfully constructed by extracting phrases from throughout the interview to say: "Kissing . . . another woman . . . in a big pool . . . of mud . . . is always something . . . I've wanted to try . . . preferably being . . . watched by . . . your readers . . . with their . . . co . . . cks out."

MISERY MEMOIRS

There's not nearly enough misery in the world, is there? Every time you turn on the news, it's nothing but sunshine and everyone laughing and people dancing with puppies and attractive old people. Sickening. If only there were some way of escaping into a world where children are made to live in the washing machine and eat nothing but sanitary products and cigarettes.

Thank jiminy, then, for misery memoirs. Which one do you

fancy? Dave Pelzer's *A Child Called It* has someone being forced naked onto a hot stove. But then *Ugly* by Constance Briscoe has bleach swallowing. You're spoiled for choice: *For Crying Out Loud: One Woman's Story of Hope and Courage; Friday's Child: What Has She Done That Is So Terrible?; The Little Prisoner: How a Childhood Was Stolen and a Trust Betrayed.* Excellent.

Some people really love their misery. Consider this Amazon customer review of Pelzer's *My Story* trilogy: "these stories will leave you sickened shocked sad crying happy thankful every feeling you could feel you get when you are reading these stories they grip you from start to end." Other misery fans are more demanding: "in 'a child called it' his mother did horrible things to him such as made him eat his own sick! but the others don't seem to be as interesting." It's so easy to play the sick-eating card too early, isn't it?

In 2003, a reformed drug addict called James Frey wrote a memoir called *A Million Little Pieces,* full of can-you-handle-it-punk accounts of his junkie hell, rendered in short, punchy, macho paragraphs.

Just.

Like.

Fucking.

HEROIN!

This.

Oprah Winfrey, who really likes misery memoirs, loved *A Million Little Pieces* and had Frey on her show so she could tell him how moved she was. Naturally, it became a best seller. But then the Smoking Gun Web site uncovered documents proving that Frey had made bits up, so it wasn't entirely real after all. There was misery in there, to feast on, but it wasn't the genuine misery suffered by another human being that people felt they were paying for when they bought into the whole thing.

Oprah invited Frey back onto the show and proceeded to tell him that he had let himself down, he had let the whole nation down, and, most heinously, he had let Oprah down. He did, it must be said, look genuinely miserable.

Maybe he'll write a memoir about it. He could call it *My Oprah Sick-Eating HEROIN Pieces.*

KATE MOSS

In the event of a nuclear war, scientists predict that only one species is guaranteed to survive unscathed: Kate Moss. She'll be scouring the post-apocalyptic tundra, cigarette in hand, looking for the hippest smoking crater around, and wishing there was just one gossip columnist left alive to report glowingly on her whereabouts.

If she just wore clothes and left it there, that would be one thing. But no, people get her to do all sorts of completely unrelated activities—like singing. Even though it is hard to see how she is better suited to making music than, say, Barry Bonds.

With grim inevitability, news of her liaison with Pete Doherty was soon followed by reports that she had been laying down some backing vocals for Babyshambles' debut album. According to reports, he thought her vocals were so good he was considering writing a duet they could sing together.

Good vocals? Are you on crack? Oh.

MOTORIST, THE, AS OPPRESSED GROUP

There is one inalienable right of man—recognized as such from ancient Greek philosophy through to the classic statements of liberal rights such as the Constitution—that today is being repressed as never before, casting a shadow over all ye who believe in Liberty. I speak, of course, of the right to drive about in a car.

How dare people like Los Angeles Mayor Antonio Villaraigosa encourage citizens to use public transportation and leave their beloved automobiles at home? Driving two blocks, alone in your car, just to buy milk is a God-given right, and one drawing on a rich tradition of political thought almost as old as man himself.

It was Aristotle who first invented the notion of "pimping" one's "ride." "These rims," he wrote, in his *Politics,* "are bitchin'."

George Washington, first president of the United States, famously said: "As Mankind becomes more liberal, they will be more apt to allow that all those who conduct themselves as worthy members of the community are equally entitled to the protections of civil government. I hope ever to see America among the foremost nations of justice and liberality. And of course to be fat and drive around in SUVs. That goes without saying."

And who can forget Teddy Roosevelt's immortal words, "Car-pool lanes are gay."

MULTIPLE-CHOICE CHRISTIAN EDUCATION SCHEMES

The Accelerated Christian Education (ACE) scheme is already widespread in all fifty states, and now is being welcomed into the fold worldwide by all sorts on the growing education/faith interface.

Why not test your knowledge against a sample question from ACE's geography exam:

1. The circumference of the Earth at the equator is 24,901.55 miles. Given this fact, what force should we let into our lives to save ourselves from eternal damnation?
a) devils
b) devils
c) devils
d) devils
e) devils
f) Jesus
g) devils
h) devils

The ACE syllabus involves learning "facts" by rote to retell "facts" in multiple-choice and fill-in-the-blanks tests. All discussion or dissent is discouraged as pupils sit in stony silence at individual desks with high dividers and work through booklets that all begin with Christian homilies. ACE students are not quite placed in a box into which voices periodically bellow, "Are you feeling the spirit of THE LORD!?" but it's not far off.

Admittedly, multiple-choice Christian Education schemes are often successfully completed by students who are otherwise unable to find their way educationally. However, this is, at least in part, because answering multiple-choice questions is easy-peasy lemon-squeezy. Particularly when one of the answers is always "Jesus."

University academics have found that successful ACE students often show no conception of independent thought; in a very real sense, it was never an option. But really, is this such a massive problem? These schools turn out orderly children with "ethos" to spare. Seriously, if hard-core Christians want to take over everything, what's the big problem? You know, apart from their urge to burn J. K. Rowling as a witch. But then, she's had it good for too long.

MUSIC SPONSORSHIP

In 2004, Britney Spears claimed that filming Pepsi's Gladiator/"We Will Rock You" ad with Beyoncé Knowles and Pink made her "feel empowered" (the campaign slogan was "Dare for More"). Later that year, Beyoncé told the press that having Destiny's Child's tour sponsored by McDonald's made them feel "truly honored." Yes, that's McDonald's, not Make-A-Wish.

Music and big business have always been curious bedfellows, but never before has the former positioned itself on the hard receiving end of things quite so readily. In 1997, when Mick Jagger really got the bandwagon rolling by jumping onstage showing off the new Rock 'N' Roll Collection of tour sponsor Tommy Hilfiger, many fans audibly gagged. But such days are long gone.

Now the stigma of being a sell-out whore has almost completely disappeared, with even nominally "noncorporate" indie bands operating on the principle, "Well, everyone else is doing it . . ." Events like the Music Upfront conference even let labels showcase forthcoming albums to corporations like Procter & Gamble, Samsung, and Mercedes for use in future ads. Co-organizing the event, Atlantic chairman Jason Flom apologized to "anyone in the ad industry who has been neglected in the past" saying: "Target your brands with our bands!"

One group who might conceivably not need the money or exposure is U2; but in interviews around their silhouette/ "Vertigo" iPod ads, the band hit new lows of twisted-logic obsequiousness. Adam Clayton called the union with Apple perfect "synergy" and Bono called the iPod "the most interesting art object since the electric guitar." At a press conference unveiling iTunes for Windows, Bono appeared on video link calling the new confluence between Microsoft and Apple "like the pope of software meeting the Dalai Lama of integration." (Don't you just love it when he says things like that? Not just that it's so appalling, but that he clearly spent *ages* thinking it up.)

If this cozy relationship really is so undemeaning, maybe Bono could consider jumping onstage wearing an iPod and phoning Steve Jobs to tell him how great iPods are before adding new lyrics to "One" about how we get to carry each other's iPods? That would be like the Babe Ruth of Messianic Twat-Rock meeting the Prince Rainier III of MP3-Playing Interface Alternatives. Or something.

"MUST-HAVE," THE PHRASE

Being told how to be hip by media planks is a constant feature of modern life. Every week, *Entertainment Weekly* publishes it's "Must List" of ten pop-culture items you must see, hear, read, or buy if you want to have any hope of surviving the next seven days. Really? If I don't check out the Clark Brothers on Fox's *The Next Great American Band,* I will die a social pariah's painful death?

Seeing certain films is "utterly essential"—with TV pundits saying things like "This is Christian Bale's year, without a doubt." Imagine having no doubts that this year, or any other year, is Christian Bale's year. What certainty!

"The FeONIC Soundbug is a must-have," we were once told by a TV "items" expert, because it turns otherwise useless flat surfaces like walls into speakers. "Flat and rigid surfaces"? Fuck 'em.

Such figures are portrayed as modern oracles peering into the misty water to somehow divine the future of thinking, being, buying. In reality, they've been sifting through a pile of press releases. Or, sometimes, looking stuff up on the Internet.

"MY LIFE AFTER . . ."

Before the age of celebrity, most would react to a painful split by staying under their bedclothes and, on reemerging, looking distant and distracted like Agnetha in late-period ABBA videos.

Thankfully, modern celebrities have now shown us the correct way to grieve over dead love: by regularly unloading into the Dictaphones of reporters for bottom-end weekly magazines about how many tears you have cried, how going to nightclubs only partially kills the pain, how your ex liked dressing up as a barrister and hanging from the banisters, how you will never watch *Laguna Beach* again, that kind of thing. At regular six-month intervals, you can join your public in "looking back at the split." Which is weird. You can stage a "joyful release" photo, like Nicole, or you can drip-feed details of your former partner's infidelities, like Jen. At some point, someone will cotton on to the idea of getting all Kate Hudson's exes together for a conference. That'd be good.

If anyone is too distraught to talk, Sis can always open up instead. When Britney Spears was too devastated to comment on her custody battle with K-Fed, *Life & Style* magazine—which we should note has neither a life nor style—instead published this quote from her sister, Jamie Lynn: "You wanted those babies, and look what you're doing! I'm glad Kevin's going to take them!" Isn't that sweet? You wish you had a sister like that.

N

NAZI HATE POP

Modern-day fascists have such poor taste in music. Anyone would think they have poor judgment generally. All that bad metal; all that *shouting*. You'd think they'd want to unwind after rupturing their rectums with all the Nazism: the marching, the bellowing ignorance, all those close-typed leaflets they hand out. But no: It's frenetic thumping and gruff slogans about white supremacy. Angry Aryans? We ask you!

One striking departure from fat, bald blokes screaming is Prussian Blue—a girl group who are a sort of Nazi version of the Olsen Twins. But where the Olsens appeal to fans of anodyne family fun, Prussian Blue appeal to fans of Aryan racial hegemony. Group members Lamb and Lynx Gaede are two blond, blue-eyed fourteen-year-olds from Bakersfield, California, who wear mini skirts and T-shirts with yellow smily faces on them (ah, cute), but the yellow smily faces are actually Hitler (oh, not so cute), complete with mustache and distinctive hairdo. (We're not making this up!) It's like Girl Power, but it's White Girl Power.

"We are proud of being white," says Lynx—unsurprising given that their shows incorporate *Sieg Heil* salutes and that one song, "Sacrifice," is dedicated to Hitler's deputy Rudolf Hess (a "man of peace who wouldn't give up").

Other top tracks are "Road to Valhalla" and "Aryan Man, Awake." Lyrics include: "Strike force! White survival. Strike force! Yeah." Gig itineraries sometimes feature Holocaust denial festivals. (How would one of those "festivals" pan out? "I don't believe the Holocaust happened." "Neither do I." "Let's get a beer." "Okay." "Is Mahmoud Ahmadinejad coming this year?" "No, he's got a cold." "Shame.")

Erich Gliebe, operator of notorious race-hate label Resistance Records, which releases Prussian Blue's efforts, believes young performers like Lynx and Lamb will expand the base of white nationalism. He said: "Eleven and twelve years old, I think that's the perfect age to start grooming kids and instill in them a strong racial identity."

Lamb and Lynx were "groomed" by their mother, April, who homeschools them using 1950s textbooks, and by their grandfather. He has a swastika on his belt buckle, on the side of his pickup truck, and registered as his cattle brand with the Bureau of Livestock Identification. (So he definitely likes swastikas. And presumably Nazi cattle.)

Lynx said: "We want to keep being white. We want our people to stay white . . . We think our race is different to other races in positive ways and that we've done more for civilization."

We must wonder, though, exactly what benefit civilization will garner from two barely pubescent girls gyrating in front of mostly male white supremacists. The target market of this pop group would appear to be Nazi pedophiles. Which even a fascist must appreciate is, in PR terms, a double-edged sword.

Nazi pedophiles: What are they like, eh?

NETWORKING

The dark art of pretending to like people in order to advance one's own self—even though that self has precisely nothing to offer the world barring an extraordinary aptitude for self-advancement.

"NOT LIKE EVERYBODY ELSE" ADVERTISING

We must not be like everybody else. We must be different. Original. And special. And we must always, *always* expect more. How do we know this? Because that's what the advertisers tell us.

"Be Original" implores Levi's. We need to go "moon-bathing," claim the ads, showing a buffed, shirtless, Levi's-wearing man balancing precariously on a moonlit rooftop. They make it look quite the thing. But if we do actually go "moon-bathing," surely we are not being "original." We are being "unoriginal." It's like jumping in the fire because a bigger boy told you to, except it's climbing around on the roof at night because Levi's told you to. Which is potentially deranged. "What, Officer? But the jeans people told me to do it!"

"There Is No Box," declares the network FX. Because their decision to air not just TV shows, but original TV shows, of both the comedy and drama variety, is so daring that clearly they're so far out of the box they can't even see that cramped square anymore! And if you watch their shows, you're out of the box, too! Good for you! Just don't leave that other box. You know, the one that glows in your living room and is called a television. Because FX kinda needs that box to survive.

When IBM used the Kinks' proto-punk anthem "I'm Not Like Everybody Else," they subverted meaning with an audacity that would make a French philosopher gasp. The song fronted the computer giant's "What Makes You Special?" campaign, which conveyed the idea that IBM was in fact an anarchist collective specifically there to cater to disaffected wild cards. Except that, in the ads, everyone was singing the anti-conformity song in perfect unison—like corporate Stepford androids. The levels of irony become so richly confusing that you start spinning out and need talking to with patience and care—to be reassured that you are, at least in some senses, like everybody else.

NOVELISTS WRITING ABOUT CURRENT AFFAIRS

Reading newspapers these days, you need some basic ground rules if you want to avoid the sudden urge to throw yourself through a window. One of the most important rules (at least of those that don't involve "Youth Correspondents") involves first scanning right down to the very end of the article. If you see there a little copyright symbol followed by the writer's name, either turn over the page or in fact drop the paper and run off into another room.

This is because, whether you've heard of them or not, the writers will be Very Important Authors. They don't usually do this sort of thing but, on this occasion, they have chosen to lower themselves from Mount Literature and walk among us. They have been touched by current events, touched in ways we normal people just wouldn't understand. There are children dying, we've all seen the pictures. But have we seen the real picture? The big picture? The picture that tells us what we're all really feeling? Probably not. After all, we're not pompous novelists straining for pseudo-profundity.

How would any of us have made sense of the horrors of

the World Trade Center attacks if it hadn't been for the likes of Salman Rushdie, Ian McEwan, and Martin Amis telling us how horrible it all was? This was, without the slightest shadow of a doubt, exactly the right time for showboating prose.

Let us consider an op-ed piece by the late Norman Mailer on our government's justification for the Iraq War: "With their dominance in sport, at work and at home eroded, Bush thought white American men needed to know they were still good at something." So powerful! So readable! So succinct! So clearly out of touch with reality! If Bush led us into Iraq to give white dudes an easy ego boost, this war is a bigger clusterfuck than we thought.

Imagine if Mailer's actual proper literary endeavors were as trite, jumped-up, and egocentric and had such little connection with reality. Surely then we'd all stop buying them? Oh, yes, that's right: They are. And we have.

NU-SNOBBERY

The poor are hilarious: Look, they don't have much money! Ha ha ha. But there's a downside, too: They sometimes have bad skin because they don't use the correct sea-salt-based exfoliant scrubs, and they can be violent. And they never appear in their own reality shows! Unless you count those Bumfights videos. And we don't. So the poor are worthless. Struggle to survive somewhere else, you dirty fucks.

O

OBITUARIES IN THE FUTURE

Scientists predict that, if the ratio of celebrities to everyone else continues increasing at the present rate, then by 2048 the size of the *New York Times* will have expanded to fill the average two-bedroom flat. The increased space will be needed to cover stories about all the new celebrities and also to report the deaths of the old ones: Sadly, Johnny Fairplay will not live forever and some poor sod will have to write his obituary.

The Paper of Record will presumably dedicate whole sections to obits for celebrities: celebrity carpenters, celebrity gardeners, celebrity dishwashers, all the entrants in all sixteen seasons of *Dancing with the Stars* (the seventeenth was canceled after the one with the 'stache out of The Killers broke his neck attempting to foxtrot), celebrity newsagents, celebrity wig makers, celebrity adult literacy tutors, and Jared from the Subway ads ("Increasingly Jared found that the only thing that helped him lose weight was crack cocaine").

Celebrity obituary writers will prepare their own obituaries. Which is poignant, in a way.

OBSERVATIONAL COMEDY

Standing on a stage. Making trite observations about everyday life. In a futile attempt to be funny. What's the deal with that? Have you seen that?

"OFFICIAL SPONSORS" OF SPORTING EVENTS

MasterCard, official sponsors of the World Cup 2006, received a lot of criticism for initially insisting that all ticket sales had to be done by extremely complicated bank transfers unless paid for by one, and only one, brand of credit card: Visa! Only joking—it was MasterCard.

Coke famously banned Pepsi products from events they sponsored. Now, you may ask what Coke is doing sponsoring sports anyway what with it making you really fat, but it's actually got quite a long tradition of sponsoring sporting events, having gotten behind the 1936 Olympics in Berlin—aka the Nazi Olympics, the one where Hitler wanted to show off Aryan superiority. Coke was pretty chummy with the Nazis generally. Indeed, Coke-staple Fanta was invented by improvising with local ingredients when the German Coke plants ran out of cola syrup during the war: They loved pop, the Nazis.

Anyway, at least Coke could argue it's an "energy" drink. What about Canon—the "official camera" of the NFL? So, in the run-up to a big game, do the players like to snap some shots for a night of post-game scrapbooking?

OPENING CEREMONIES

Great international sporting events like the Olympics and the World Cup are designed to bring people across the world together, to realize briefly our underlying commonality. And the opening ceremonies do indeed unite all the corners of the world with the same thought: *Just fucking get on with it.* And also: *Where did they get all that material?*

Wherever the host nation, these gaudy displays of national pride always look like a school special assembly with serious money to burn. But there are moments to cherish: there's the grandeur in Bob Costas's voice as he reads from the script: "And now . . . here come the grape pickers . . . in their traditional costume . . . picking their grapes . . . from the grapevines . . . on the hillsides." Or there's his mute disbelief at the sight of Björk dressed as an ocean singing about sweat.

The transcendent opening ceremony moment of recent years occurred at the opening of the 2002 Winter Olympics at Bonneville when each country was introduced with a short rhyming couplet—in French and English. One particularly memorable example went: "They come from a land that's long and hilly/Welcome to the gallant athletes from Chile."

ORGANIC CONSUMER SCAMS

If you buy organic produce from abroad, and the organic produce has been transported by plane, then that organic produce, far from being an in-touch-with-nature, straight-from-the-soil bundle of environmental goodness, will have probably burned its own weight in aviation fuel to get here (as part of a larger consignment; you don't get kiwi fruits individually flying themselves here from New Zealand).

The ethical farming group Sustain analyzed a sample basket of twenty-six imported organic goodies. They found it had traveled a distance equivalent to six times around the equator

(150,000 miles), a journey that will have released as much CO_2 as a four-bedroom household cooking meals for eight months. But the supermarkets know that the little ORGANIC sticker means more money for them, so they really could not care less about jet-set comestibles.

It hurts to say this, but if you want to go organic, you might have to end up dealing with hippies. Farming is the only area of life where hippies are best. You never hear about hippie builders, say—oh, we got some hippies in to do the extension and they were really good.

For farming, though, we're with the hippies. It's either them or you end up with subsidy-guzzling reactionaries who fuck foxes. That's the impression we get, anyway.

OSCARS, THE

Another year on and Hollywood's managed to turn out, what, maybe *three* decent films? That's right, give yourselves a big clap. Funny how you never seem to win awards in competitions not run by yourselves.

OSCAR PARTIES

So many parties, so little talent. There's Barry Diller's pre-Oscar luncheon, CAA agent Bryan Lourd's day-before shindig, the Weinstein Company's Saturday bash, the Governor's Ball, *InStyle*'s viewing party at Republic, and—of course—the *Vanity Fair* soiree at Morton's.

They all sound amazing, except for the fact that you are not allowed to get pissed ("You just want to have a celebratory glow," says one insider), there's never enough room ("There's never enough room," says another insider), and if you're not either a mogul or someone involved in a nominated film, no one will be that interested in talking to you. Says yet another insider: "If you're not one of those people, you're always looking around wondering, 'Who do I know, who do I talk to, why am I here?' "

Of course, the party to be seen at is always Elton John's party. Everyone simply has to get into Elton's party. If you aren't at Elton's party, you don't want to know about Elton's party. You will choke. You'll just die. You *have* to be there. Nobody who is there can even bear to tell others who aren't there how good it is: That's how good it is. Actually, an insider has spilled the beans: "It was lovely, lots of margaritas." What time is the party? Margarita time.

We do not understand this. How is Elton John, now, in the twenty-first century, still the celebrity hub around which revolves whole other galaxies of vain, vacuous fluff? He had some hits in the 1970s. Then there was *The Lion King*. And what else? Is it a Diana thing? What?

This is supposed to be Hollywood. You know, the shining city on the hill; homeless runaways being lured into the porn industry; "It was just the pictures that got small"; complicated young people with a whole set of personalities . . . Have they not seen those photos of Captain Fantastic in the duck outfit?

To us, it's not screaming Rita Hayworth.

OVERSTIMULATED CHILDREN

Are your children mural artists? No. So do not encourage them to draw on the fucking walls. If they must display an artistic bent, simply supply them with a piece of paper. Or a canvas.

Try to find a happy medium between fucking them up—you may not mean to, but you do—and letting them trash other people's houses. No one wants a miniature rampant id crashing around their house, drawing on it.

According to many reports, children are increasingly brought up to believe they are the last in line of the Ming dynasty. Recent studies show that middle-class parents are creating a new generation of "brat bullies." Apparently, some parents are unwilling to curb their children's desires, believing this would stifle their creativity. These worshipped little gods "expect all the teachers and other kids to kowtow to them. If they don't, they start to bully the other children."

P

PANDA DIPLOMACY

In this ever-changing world in which we live, communication is more important than ever. Which is why all efforts to step up diplomacy are now so imperative. The pandas are on board. Are you?

In January 2006, the deputy secretary of state assigned to manage U.S. relations with China, Robert Zoellick, entered the seemingly cuddly, but actually rather prickly, world of panda diplomacy.

Asked to meet a prize cub, he acknowledged to reporters that he and his aides had pondered any message the image might convey. They had discussed the various inferences that could be drawn from several panda poses before agreeing to "take Jing Jing on his lap."

We, too, share doubts about what message this pose might convey. "You want to know how the panda felt?" Zoellick asked reporters. "Very soft."

In fact, panda diplomacy is among the more treacherous forms of diplomacy. In 2005, Taiwan was offered two pandas by the Chinese Communist Party. The panda diplomacy, in this case, was backed by hundreds of missiles pointed at Taiwan across the hundred-mile channel that separates the island from China. So accepting the pandas meant subconsciously acquiescing to Chinese domination: "Look, pandas! Accept Chinese rule. Aren't they cute? What did I just say? Oh, nothing. Accept Beijing's divine diktat. Aaah, pandas . . ."

When Taiwan understandably hesitated, the *China Daily* newspaper painted President Chen as "bellicose" in his opposition to the "peaceful pandas." The editorial ran: "Stubborn as he is, Chen has to face the reality: he may be able to block the entry of the panda couple but he cannot stop the Taiwanese people's love for the pandas."

Frustrated with some of the media's coverage, Jan Jyh-horng, secretary general of Taiwan's Mainland Affairs Council, argued that "pandas are not communists." That is true. Pandas tend to fall into one of two camps: They are either instinctively in favor of bringing about greater redistribution of wealth by reform of the capitalist system from within; or they advocate a simple life based on anarchist collectives, which admittedly is communistic, but certainly not in any sense akin to Stalinist-style "communism." How do we know this? We asked one.

Want to know how it felt? Very soft.

PANINIS

Panini was once simply an Italian sticker company selling packets of cartoon character cards from small boxes situated by the counter in a card store. Then it went into the cheese toastie market and really cleaned up.

It was so successful, in fact, that it overreached itself and ran out of bread, so it started to make its cool, continental snacks out of cardboard instead. It also didn't have time to print the standard warning on the side of the packet: "Do not under any circumstances heat this fucker to 400°F as that is hot enough to melt the inside of someone's head."

In Milan, no one would serve you a Caesar salad panini straight from a lovingly sealed polythene bag that is now practically on fucking fire. Unless, for some reason, they hated your family. Hot leaves? Bubbling hot yellow sauce? This is not the Italian way.

Breakfast paninis with scrambled egg? Balls to them.

PAP PICS OF CELEB KIDS WITH THEIR FACES BLOCKED OUT

Here's Angelina walking Maddox up to school. But look, we respect their privacy, so we've made little Maddy's face all squarey so he looks like a victim of crime. But he's holding his thumbs aloft, so he must be all right. Look at the caption: "Thumbs up—shows he's happy." See?

But should his thumbs have been pixelated, too? You don't want his face growing up perfectly well adjusted while his thumbs turn into really weird digits, all warped by the strains of celebrity. Have the boy's thumbs not the right to privacy?

Or maybe we're missing something and celebrities just have children with really blurred faces.

PAYING OFF YOUR MORTGAGE IN TWO YEARS

With house prices now being set by absinthe-crazed madmen throwing dice at each other, people are taking out 35-, 40-, even 45-year mortgages. But you can do it in two.

Saving pennies makes dollars, so if you save a lot of pennies, well, there you go, you've paid off your mortgage. It's all about tightening your belt here and there. To the point where your waist measurement is the same as your shoe size.

Money-saving tips in these kinds of books include stopping smoking (they all add up, and are bad for you anyway), not buying coffee (instead, go to places where they give you free coffee), and, if you must buy things, getting them on the Internet (it's slightly cheaper!). Be careful, though. One top tip warns: "If foraging or looking for food in the wild, make sure you properly identify safe foodstuffs." So try to avoid toadstools and deadly nightshade if you can. The road to early mortgage repayment is full of victims who, rather than shedding the dark cloak of mortgage, had their stomach pumped after munching the wrong kind of toadstool.

But even this is amateur child's play to the King of the Saving of the Pennies, financial writer Cliff D'Arcy. If saving pennies were a sparky young lady with excellent conversation, he would be her Mr. D'Arcy, Cliff D'Arcy. He's the sort of guy who thinks lying down in a darkened room is wasteful.

In July 2006, Mr. D'Arcy announced in a promotional e-mail sent out by popular financial Web site the Motley Fool that he was about to embark on a period of "Extreme Budgeting": "In January of this year, my discretionary spending came to less than $15, which is a new personal best . . . [Now] I plan to steer clear of alcohol, cigarettes, drinks and snacks, fast food and takeaways, with my only treat being a weekend newspaper or two . . . I appreciate that extreme budgeting isn't everyone's cup of tea, because it is a tough test of willpower."

Speaking of tea, Mr. D'Arcy signed off: "I'm off to have a nice cup of tea, which is my only vice during my (financial) detox month!" Presumably reusing the bag for the twentieth time. Possibly a bag that came from the Red Cross.

Putting aside minor worries that money is just a chimerical, abstract way of exchanging goods, services, and human effort, and that this might be an utter waste of miserable time that involves actively hegemonizing yourself with the mores of Mammon, I have created my own "Very Extreme Indeed and Certainly More Extreme Than the Motley Fool's, Which Isn't Extreme at All . . . In Fact They Are Just Pussies: I Could Pay Off My Mortgage in Three Months, No Bother—What Do You Think of That? Budget."

Take all of the measures we have listed here and you could be saving—quite literally—in the region of $200 or even $300 *every single year:*

1. Swap credit card and utility companies to get the best deals. Switch companies anything up to four or even five times a day. By really staying alert, you can save well over a whole entire dollar each and every week. Some people might argue that if you expended the same amount of effort working, you would make considerably more, but screw them. They don't know.
2. Don't piss your money up against a wall. I get tired of endlessly telling people that if they keep going to bars, buying beer, and generally enjoying themselves, they will inevitably have less money than they might otherwise have had. Why can't they just suck on the juicy beer mats provided at the bar? Money's going in one end and getting pissed out the other. Unless you can find me someone who will pay for piss, I'm not interested. And you won't. Because that doesn't happen. A piss merchant, buying and sell-

ing piss—it's a fucking stupid idea. (If you do ever come across somewhere with a piss merchant, let me know.)

3. You should always—*always*—only use financial products you've never heard of. If you've heard of an ISA, you need a cash ISA. If you've heard of a cash ISA, you need a mini cash ISA. If you've heard of a mini cash ISA, you need to call the Bank de Bank, Zurich, and ask for Juan. Say you need "a dirty one." The code word is *"flaps."* You'll also be wanting a PEP, a PAP, the PUP, and a PARP. Don't forget to claim your allowances for those, either, like some sort of ass-clown.
4. Boil up some grass to make grassy stew. Eat stuff out of bins.
5. Sell your toenails on eBay (what are they actually *for,* anyway?).
6. Never. Ever. Do. Anything. Ever. At all.
7. Help us.
8. Kill yourself. There's no surer way to spend less than being dead. As a bonus, any insurance policies you hold will be paying out like a fruit machine with three triple bars on hold—not that we'd know about that, not risking our precious pennies on such atrocious frivolities. Irony is free—so treat yourself to a highly poignant death by smashing your brains open against the window of your bank. (If you bank online—which we would advise; there are some great deals out there—just go to the nearest branch of the bank of which your online account supplier is a subsidiary.) Now, for insurance reasons, it needs to look like an accident. You'll need a big run-up to get enough force to kill yourself, so start from the other side of the road while looking down the street and smiling and

waving into the distance, as if you have just seen an old friend or acquaintance and have become distracted. Just keep running until you hit the bank and hopefully die. Remember to run very fast or you won't get enough force to kill yourself. No one wants to come around outside Citibank with blood from their own head smeared down the windows. Also remember, in the days leading up to killing yourself, that you can save money by not eating anything or turning on any lights.

PENIS ENLARGEMENT E-MAILS

Ca:nYo:uLea:veMeAl:one:I'mQu:iteH:ap:pyWit:hMyDi:ck TheWa:yIt:Is:AndEv:enIfIWasn'tD:oYouRea:llyThi:nkI'dWant: It:ToGetC:utOpenBySo:meBa:sta:rdSpamme:rs?

PEOPLE IN BEAR COSTUMES ON MOTORBIKES ADVERTISING STUFF

Happens more than you might imagine.

PICTURES OF CLUBBERS

As in, people gyrating at the camera used to illustrate listings and/or articles about clubs. You'd think that if people were off their faces, they might consider staying away from the camera lens, what with being off your face not usually considered to be a good look for your face. But no.

It's been a staple now for about twenty years: loads of faces, off their faces. Holding on to their mates, waving a drink about, throwing their hands in the air. Why the fuck would anyone want to see this picture? We weren't there. We probably don't wish we had been there. If we are going to see pictures of people fucked out of their minds in a nightclub, please have the decency to make them members of the Bush family. Or high-ranking television personalities.

On the odd occasion that we buy *Dazed & Confused* magazine by accident—which, by the way, claims to be a journal of "ideas"—the photos in the back of some hip schmoozathon or other always, *always* include the same hairy, muttonchopped Japanese man holding a beer bottle. It doesn't seem to matter where the party is—New York, Paris, wherever. He really gets around.

We don't know what that's about.

PLASTIC SURGERY FOR PETS

Joke corner: "My dog's got no nose." "Really?" "Yes, I had it chopped off because I didn't like the way it looked."

Cutting bits off your pet is all the rage, with some California vets even pointing to potential health benefits. Dogs with floppy ears need them clipped because they are more prone to inflammation from the "buildup of moisture" (oh, and they can't hear as well—but they don't know that). Docking a dog's tail is highly practical because, according to one American Kennel Club judge, "people can't grab the tail." No, not if it hasn't got one.

Dogs can even be debarked by removing two folds of tissue on either side of their larynx. When these folds come together, the standard dog makes that woofing noise we tend to associate with dogs. Whip his folds out and, when he goes to bark, he produces a whisper, like a bark heard far away, when (get this) he's still right next to you! Obviously no one likes a mental nonstop barking dog, but a spooky whispering one that sounds like he's down the road doesn't feel like much of a step up.

POLE-DANCING LESSONS

The Australian Family Association became outraged when children as young as seven began taking "pole fitness classes," in which they use poles to perform strengthening and flexibility exercises. Said the group's spokeswoman Angela Conway, "There are plenty of exercise tools out there. Why choose a pole, the classic phallic symbol of the pornographic world?"

Fucking killjoys. Pole dancing's just a great way of working out—and it's fun! It's like Pilates for women who think: *Let's play at being sex workers!*

Top pole-dancing teachers Polestars assure us: "Lessons are for fun, not professional training. All classes are a man-free zone!" This is a grave disappointment to many women who were actually hoping to spend their leisure hours swinging about for the delectation of drunken businessmen jiggling their hands around in their suit-trouser pockets.

Now, Polish dancing lessons—they get you really fit.

POLICEMEN CUTTING UP DEAD PEOPLE ON TELEVISION

Incessant.

POLITICIANS' "SEXUAL AURA"

When George Bush paraded about the deck of the SS *Abraham Lincoln* in a battle flight suit in May 2003 to pronounce the war in Iraq "over," many descriptions came to mind. For most of us, "hottie" probably wasn't one of them—although it was for some maniac from the *Wall Street Journal.* Meanwhile, Republican speechwriter Peggy Noonan said she half expected Bush to "tear open his shirt and reveal the big S on his chest." *S* for Shitty Shithead Shitforbrains, presumably.

In the 2004 U.S. election, Bush and Kerry tried to target the key undecided constituency of single women voters with their "sex appeal." Surely they would both have been better served targeting "people with goose fat where their brains should be," rather than conjuring up terrifying visions of them having a wet-trunks contest.

And really, what's so bleeding studdish about Bill Clinton? Granted, he doesn't have buck teeth or a goiter, but that doesn't mean he's someone you'd want to see in the buff, aroused.

Something has really gone wrong with your attitudes to sex if you want to whisper sweet nothings to Mike Huckabee or suck off Joe Biden. What next? Pieces eulogizing the blubbery intensity of Dennis Hastert? Ah, but when you meet him . . .

PORN, MISLEADING USE OF THE WORD

Porn gets everywhere these days. Even where it patently is not. (See **Calamity Porn.**)

We are now seduced with "gardening porn" (porn involving hostas), "car porn" (porn involving NASCAR), "gadget porn" (porn with Inspector Gadget), and "gastro porn" (belly porn). Anyone thinking one of these items would feature something of a stimulating bent might have been disappointed to see an older man—probably wearing a sweater—discussing the cons of arborvitae or prosciutto or something. That's not porn. Or, if it is, only a tiny minority will get their rocks off over it.

It's surprising they don't trail the news as "topico-porn."

And the weather could be called "Hot 'n' Wet."

Maybe it could be introduced: "Now here's Peter with some hot fucking."

PORSCHE SUVS

Want an SUV so you can loom over other road users like the U.S. Army? But also want something sporty to accelerate ludicrously away from the lights before suddenly braking at the next roundabout?

Then the Porsche Cayenne is the car for you: two utterly pointless vehicles in one. No one likes you.

POWER LISTS

Every magazine now has a "Power 100," from *Forbes* to *Accountancy Age* to the *Frog Hollow PTA Newsletter*. It's so devalued the ranking of "#1 Most Grand Poobah" that *Entertainment Weekly*—annually home to its own Hollywood-centric Power List—instead created a "Smart List" in 2007, recognizing the fifty most intelligent people in the industry, because, quote, "It's not about power anymore—meet the brains who are taking the film biz forward."

Please, like brains ever have power. You'll never top *Vanity Fair*'s "Power List of Power Lists" with that attitude.

POWERPOINT

The Microsoft tool that encourages people to think and talk like fuckheads.

PRICE PROMISES

Now, surely, if you were going to hike around town/the Net checking whether somewhere else sells this item cheaper, you'd do it *before coming in here to buy it and not afterward like some sort of twat.*

PRINCE ANDREW

In 2003, the fourth in line to the throne decided to travel from London to a lunch engagement in Oxford by chartered helicopter at a cost to the taxpayer of almost $6,000. When faced with complaints about squandering the public purse, a palace spokeswoman explained that reliability was paramount as the Oxford date was a state banquet in honor of Vladimir Putin. Sadly, "setting out earlier" was, she continued, simply not possible as there was "something he'd forgotten to do" and also "something on the telly."

Prince Andrew loves helicopters so much that, when no helicopter can be found for him, he scampers up and down the palace corridors shouting: "Mummy! Copter! Mummy! Copter!"

PRODUCT, THE WORD

"What products do you use?"

"Oh, you know . . . pens, ball bearings, all sorts."

"No, I mean beauty products."

"Oh, sorry. You needed to be more specific. And less of a fucking prick."

PROPERTY LADDER

A marvelous system that separates society into two camps: the smug and the damned.

PUBLIC BATHROOMS, LACK OF

Thank God for McDonald's. As a pleasing bonus, when you relieve yourself in McDonald's without purchasing one of their special patties of death, you are quite literally taking the piss out of them. Actually, no—you're quite literally giving piss to them. Anyway, they don't like it.

Starbucks are also very handy for a wiz-and-run. And bars. Except the one I popped into in Brooklyn in 2001 where the burly landlord made me buy a shot on reappearance from the can on pain of a punch in the face. The fat bastard.

PUBLIC PHONE BOOTHS, STATE OF

Will no one think of the junkies?

Q

"QUALITY" HOLLYWOOD MOVIES

People often stereotype Hollywood as a machine always preying on our basest needs for violence, sex, and glamour. It's not, though, sadly. It tries being deep, too, which, when it comes to making films, is something that is best left to the Europeans. Except the British.

These films can generally be spotted by any sign of the following: Sam Mendes; Jude Law doing an American accent; Kevin "I love the theater best" Spacey; Spielberg and Hanks! Together again!; a "normal" middle-American suburb where everything is not as it seems; Gwyneth Paltrow playing a famous poet; Nicole Kidman playing a famous author (with a big nose); lives being changed forever by a car accident; Paul Haggis; and Sam Mendes and Paul Haggis! Together again!

QUESTIONING WHETHER GEORGE CLOONEY IS REAL

"He acts, he directs, he's gorgeous, he's intelligent, he's politically committed: can he be real?!"

It will no doubt relieve the redoubtable Mr. Clooney that we have an answer to that question.

And the answer is "Yes." Isn't it obvious? Look at him!

QUICK RECIPES

By strange coincidence, the craze for cooking fancy food has coincidentally coincided with the craze for working into the evening and then feeling the need to pass out from drink. This has led to a craze for quick recipes.

So all food magazines advertise the "Quick and Easy" aspect of their "Tried & Tested Recipes." (What, you've actually tried out the recipes? With this trying and testing, you are really spoiling us.)

In his book *Jamie's Dinners,* British chef Jamie Oliver claims that, in the past fifteen years, the average time spent making a meal for the family has slipped from an hour to thirteen minutes. He then describes some extremely quick "Five Minute Wonders," a section that should more accurately be called: "Five Minutes, My Giddy Sweet Back Bottom." He even adds a challenge: "Each recipe has the time it took for me to make it—you never know, you might be able to beat me on some of them!"

Well, *you* try making beef with pak choi, mushrooms, and noodles, for instance—which can apparently be done and dusted with coriander in five minutes twelve seconds, including slicing the red onion, slicing the ginger, finely slicing the chile, brushing and tearing up the mushrooms, and quartering the pak choi—without slicing the tops of your fingers clean off and leaving the kitchen a blood-spurting mess. Particularly when you've been drinking.

Really, your partner might as well have the car running for that mercy dash to the ER. Is this what he wants? Emergency wards full of wannabe quick chefs! Is this part of his bold vision for public-sector renewal? And your partner's in no fit state to drive a car—they've been drinking. Look at the fucking state of them!

Honestly, he comes across as such a saint. But really he's still a bastard.

R

R&B BALLADS

That is not an album. That is somewhere in the region of one decent fast song followed by thirty tons of Disney-does-gospel-with-satin-sheets-in-hell mush with no discernible words except "Woh-oh-oh-oh-aaaaaahhh! Ooooooh! Oooaoaoaoaoaoa! Aaargh! Aaargh! Aargh! Yooo-hooo!"

And those aren't even real words. Bullshit, really.

RAZOR BLADES THAT CAN SHAVE EVEN CLOSER THAN THE HITHERTO CLOSEST-SHAVING BLADE, WHICH WAS ALREADY REALLY QUITE CLOSE

Shaving has certainly come on in leaps and bounds since men dragged flinty bits of flint down their hirsute faces, pulling out clumps of hair matted with animal fat and their own fetid blood. "Aaaarrrggggghhhhh!" they would say. "For fucking fuck's sake. That really hurt and now it's all stingy and raw and throbbing and raw."

Then there were the so-called cutthroat razors, but these took a dive in popularity after barbers started cutting people up and putting them in pies. That's when the safety razor was invented by King Camp Gillette, in 1895. (Hur hur, King Camp. He's called King Camp.)

And bang! The race was on—to make the safety razor bigger, better, closer, and, crucially, more expensive. Along came lubricant strips and "spring loading," "open cartridge architecture," and handles with "knurled elastomeric crescents." First there was one blade, then there were two. Then there were three, then—you can see where this is going. Now there are five—yes, five. Count 'em. And weep.

The new Gillette innovation has five razor blades in it. *Five.* Not four—like the Wilkinson Sword Quattro—but five. Five. Can't you count? We said five. It's very exciting.

Now, some people might suggest it's probably impossible to get closer than existing razors in a way perceptible to the naked eye. They might say it's a colossal waste of a billion dollars and the full-time efforts of a hundred people to go around developing new five-blade razors like the old ones were going out of fashion, which they are. Perhaps these people would agree with Roger Hamby, of the Cutlery & Allied Trades Research Association, who said: "The Holy Grail of closeness was reached thirty years ago with the first twin-blade razors." But what do "some people" know?

The names of these babies alone should be enough to reassure us of their scientific veracity and general goodness. Sensor—you know what it's all about. Mach 3—the blade so manly, it has a name vaguely reminiscent of strafing Afghan villages. Mach 3 Turbo—it vibrates! Mach 3 Turbo G-force! (Don't know what that one does.) The five-blader, which has seventy-five patents on it and is made in a Class 5000 clean room in Berlin, an environment purer than an operating theater, is called Fusion. Yes, it has capacities so mind boggling it can only be described by conjuring up the spirit of jazz rock. Dark magus!

READY MEALS

Should you stray off the modern food-Nazi holy-eating track for a sneaky fix of bubbling additive paste, you might need to develop the appetite of a particularly picky three-year-old. Because these things really ought to be called ready-for-another-meal-in-an-incredibly-short-space-of-time meals. Or "snacks," as we believe such meager portions were termed in the olden days.

For this reason, "Where's the rest of my fucking ready meal, you chiseling shysters!?" is a phrase that should be heard shouted by disgruntled customers at supermarkets throughout the land as they stomp down the aisles, pushing over stacks of promotional Pringles and turning off the fridges.

"Serves 2"! Serves two *what,* exactly? Cockatiels?

I HAVE GIVEN YOU FOUR BUCKS AND NINETY-NINE CENTS—AND I *DEMAND* SUSTENANCE!

RECRUITMENT VIDEOS

In the War on Terror, the recruitment videos of the opposition have the considerable advantage of a medieval fundamentalist ideology to fall back on. A tack that sadly isn't available to the U.S. Army.

The recruiters' job has traditionally involved making joining up seem like a "fun" and "exciting" thing for go-getting youngsters to do. Admirably, they don't attempt to hoodwink youngsters into thinking that war is just a large-scale computer game. Oh no, that's wrong: Visit www.americasarmy.com to play the only online, multiplayer video game "Based on the Experience of Real U.S. Army Soldiers" and sponsored by the U.S. Army.

Unfortunately for the recruiters, though, the "fun" side of being a soldier is still difficult to convey. The new ads focus on the less war-like aspects of joining the army ("It's not all gun-related mayhem; sometimes it's preparing breakfast, too"). But sadly, in times of war, one inescapable fact of army life is—yes, that's right—war. It just keeps cropping up.

RESTAURANT SERVICE CHARGES

Different from a tip in several key ways: It's not voluntary and it doesn't often get to the staff. Many establishments either split the service charge with the staff or just keep it all for themselves. So it's not even a "service" charge, a charge in appreciation of the staff, who might reasonably expect to get paid properly anyway. It's just a charge: someone asking you for extra money for no reason whatsoever, which they will then simply keep. You can see why they don't call it that on the menu.

RESTAURANT SERVICE CHARGES THAT ONLY APPLY TO PARTIES OF MORE THAN TEN PEOPLE

More service, certainly, but only because there is more stuff *being served.* You thieving shits.

RESTAURANTS THAT REFILL HEINZ BOTTLES WITH CHEAPER KETCHUP

You're not fooling anyone.

RESTAURANTS WITH UNFEASIBLY SMALL TOILETS

As you squeeze between the door and sink into a cubicle that was last cleaned—that is, given a cursory wipe with a damp toilet roll—sometime in the latter half of the twentieth century, note how the extra table space in this Indian/greasy spoon/Chinese restaurant created by making the unfeasibly small toilet into which you are now trying to pry yourself so unfeasibly small is *never* occupied by a diner. It will *always* be either empty or occupied by restaurant staff smoking cigarettes.

Sometimes these restaurants exude an air of genuine tragedy and thwarted ambition. This expresses itself in the need to walk a very long way to reach the unfeasibly small toilet. You must travel either upstairs or downstairs, through the never-used overflow room, full of piled-up tables once upon a time destined for office holiday parties that never came. These rooms often manage simultaneously to smell musty but also smell of paint, even though nothing that could rationally be described as "decorating" has ever taken place there.

And there you are, in the semi-darkness, a bit drunk, tripping balls on MSG, wading through this shrine to the Unknown Diner, this culinary purgatory, Godot's own bistro—just to piss in a cupboard.

RESTUARANTS WITHOUT TOILETS

Basically, what they're saying is: "We've had your money, but we've not got a pot for *you* to piss in—now buzz off. And once you have buzzed off, go and fuck yourself."

CONDOLEEZZA RICE

Oil giant Chevron loves its former executive Condi Rice so much, it named an oil tanker after her. How truly awful must you be for the oil industry to like you that much?

When news of this homage caused controversy, the company quietly renamed the ship. The name they chose instead was *Condoleezza Rice? Oil-Loving Secretary of State Who Oversees the Invasion of Middle Eastern Countries to Privatize Their Oil Infrastructure for Use by U.S. Oil Giants? Never Heard of Her! We Did Once Know Somebody Called Condoleezza Rice, But Not That One.*

Everyone always goes on about Condoleezza Rice's supposed "cleverness." But she herself rates George W. Bush as "someone of tremendous intellect"—so the bar has been set quite low here. Let's hope she never gets a job as, say, a college professor, because that could blow her mind.

Rice did attend the University of Denver at the age of fifteen—but it was only to study the piano. And that is not, let's face it, a proper subject. Neither does it prepare you for high office: No one's going to look to Billy Joel in a crisis, are they? Not unless it somehow involves capturing Captain Jack or drinking loads of wine.

RICH, THE

The sumptuous invitation cards read:

> From the château steeped in history,
> We enter a world of maharajahs and mystery,
> A gilded palace from Bikaner brings,
> A lavish feast fit for a king.

The "king" was steel magnate Lakshmi Mittal, the richest man in Britain and the third richest in the world. The "château" was the finest in France, Vaux le Vicomte, on the banks of the Seine. The "lavish feast" was the June 2004 wedding of Mittal's daughter Vanisha, which lasted for six days. India's finest chefs were flown in, and Kylie Minogue performed; there was a live Bollywood extravaganza about the happy couple. Fireworks exploded in every direction, lighting up the whole of Paris.

The feast certainly was "lavish." Over thirty million dollars' worth of "lavish." We think the point they were trying to make was: "We—let's not beat around the bush here—are the dog's very rich bollocks." Mittal couldn't flaunt his wealth more if he flew over the poorer quarters of Mumbai in a helicopter shouting through a megaphone: "You, yes you there—I am rich and you are poor. Look at me, up here, the rich bloke in the helicopter. Yes, me—Mr. Moneybags here. Do not look at you, who is poor, look at me, who is rich."

Fans of the rich, the kind of people who want to press their nose against the Mittals' glass and marvel at the shiny objects—people such as the author of the recent book *Rich Is Beautiful*—often invoke the so-called trickle-down effect, whereby the great wealth of a tiny minority, despite them apparently spending it on gilded palaces and lavish feasts, is quietly and invisibly percolating down to the rest of us. We're not sure how: Maybe they hide coins down the back of single mothers' sofas?

Whether their blood is blue or red, the one thing that unites everyone rich is, of course, really, really, really hating taxes. You'd think that as all the super-rich's super-riches are generated by the whole of society (and with the trickle-down effect turning out to be a little, well, "inefficient"), governments might risk slightly offending the delicate sensibilities of the rich by inquiring if, after all, they might like to, you know, pay some fucking taxes?

Even a tiny increase would raise sums so large the IRS would run out of carrier bags to put it in. That way, the wealth could go directly into things like education, culture, health care, that sort of thing; steering it ever so slightly away from bank accounts in tax havens and sweetmeats for a clique of rapacious, parasitical, reductive, generally unpleasant shits.

If only it were that simple. George Bush has found that, although clearly they'd love to tax the rich, it is a physical impossibility. Even if the rich didn't "move abroad," there still wouldn't be any surplus billions heading toward society's coffers. Bush explained: "The really rich people figure out how to dodge taxes." Blair claimed that if top-rate taxes were raised, "Large numbers of those taxpayers—probably the wealthiest—would simply hire a whole lot of new accountants to do this and that."

Compared with, say, using military might to recast entire societies in parts of the globe where everyone hates them, this man considers that closing a few tax loopholes would be "too difficult." Suicidal jihadists? Bring 'em on.

Accountants? Accountants doing "this and that"? To the boats! To the boats!

KEITH RICHARDS

Keef is the original punk. The everlasting renegade pirate outlaw riffmeister. In a world of fakes, the Stones' legendary guitarist is the real deal, the keeper of the flame. Except, erm, he's a pampered old jet setter and a very silly man who was recently beaten up by an errant coconut.

The road of excess is meant to lead to the palace of wisdom. In Keef's case, it has led to the palace of tottering about playing the same riff for thirty years with a scarf tied around your head. Is that wisdom? Shouldn't have thought so. Wise men don't snort their dad's ashes.

But millions believe Keith has lived the rock 'n' roll dream so they don't have to. For them, personal nirvana would be to party with Keef back in the day. Even though partying with Keef back in the day would generally have involved watching someone fall asleep and drool and then wondering if he's started turning blue or if that's just the light. The rock 'n' roll thing to say is that the Stones are "his band," that Mick is just his singer. In which case, why does this renowned renegade let "his band" tour the world sponsored by T-Mobile? Or cancel a string of UK dates because they were worried about paying more taxes? That certainly doesn't sound very rock.

Keef is the fearless spirit who said: "If you're going to kick authority in the teeth, you might as well use two feet." But, in living memory, the only "authority" Keith has kicked with two feet is the Ramblers' Association. In 2002, he won his long-running battle to move a footpath farther away from his West Sussex mansion—even though it was already separated by a thick hedge and a moat.

Thankfully, Keith's lawyers took on the Ramblers on his behalf. Nevertheless, Keith prides himself on being A Bit Tasty—and, to be fair, he is fairly dangerous. But only in that he's an addled old soak who insists on carrying concealed knives. While drunk. During sessions for the 1983 Stones album *Undercover,* the guitarist would emphasize any point by swishing a swordstick. People said this was "cool" when what they should have said was: "Come on, Keith. Don't be such a schmuck all the time."

ROADTANKS—SUVS, 4X4S, ETC.

Market researchers are good. The ones employed by the U.S. car industry found that people who buy SUVs are insecure, anti-social fucks who couldn't give a beggar's testicle about their fellow man: And who'd have worked that out on their own?

Here's what Keith Bradsher of the *New York Times* reports the U.S. auto industry says about 4x4 drivers: "They tend to be people who are insecure and vain. They are frequently insecure about their marriages and uncomfortable about parenthood. They often lack confidence in their driving skills. Above all, they are apt to be self-centered and self-absorbed, with little interest in their neighbors and communities." No way! If pushed, the head of General Motors would say they are "fucking turds." Probably. He'd certainly think it. Probably.

4x4s are just a way of saying: "My family's got a big cock."

They are a marvel of science and technology, though: When we were kids, they only had 2x4s, and they were just pieces of wood. You couldn't off-road on them, not even in Alabama. So things have certainly come on in leaps and bounds since then.

Amazing, science and technology, isn't it? Last winter, we gave some friends toe warmers. They're little sticky gel packs you stick to the outside of your socks and—get this!—even though they are cold when you take them out of the packet, stick them to your socks and they go all hot and keep your feet toasty. Now, how does that work if not by sorcery? By science and technology, that's how. Or it could be sorcery. We don't actually know.

ROMANTIC COMEDIES

"I really loved *Maid in Manhattan*" is a phrase one never hears. Or "I really loved that film *Wimbledon*." This is because romantic comedies are commissioned on the basis of a six- or eight-word premise, which then everyone who is involved neglects to expand into an actual script. Com does not ensue. Nor does rom.

The king of such films is Matthew McConaughey, a man who can smirk quizzically in posters next to Jennifer Lopez or smirk quizzically in posters next to Sandra Bullock. He was recently seen smirking quizzically in posters next to Sarah Jessica Parker for *Failure to Launch:* She's falling in love, but he still lives with his parents! Oh, and he's a boat broker, hence the title—it's applicable both to his familial situation and to the boats that, as a boat broker, he brokes. It's almost like literature.

Here's Matthew McConaughey on the difficulty of finding the right motivation for his romcom characters: "Sometimes, in a romantic comedy, the male is sometimes the foil—meaning do I pull to the left? Do I pull to the right? Which way do I go? I don't know what to do!"

Coming soon: *Staying Away from the Herd.* Wealthy socialite Jennifer Garner is smitten after meeting Matthew McConaughey at a high-class masquerade, but then she discovers he's not a Wall Street banker but herds cattle. Can this relationship ever be a dung deal? You'll be laughing till the . . . well, you know.

McConaughey on the chemistry between himself and leading ladies such as Kate Hudson, his co-star in *How to Lose a Guy in 10 Days:* "If you've got chemistry, you kind of know what's going to happen, but you enjoy going along for the ride . . . We have similar senses of humor, man. Sometimes I do things that she doesn't think are funny, but she's laughing because I think they're funny while sometimes she'll do things that I don't think are funny, but I'm cracking up because she thinks it's funny."

Coming soon: *She's So My Dad's Date.* Matthew McConaughey plays the son of aging womanizer Sean Connery. There's trouble in the family when son falls for father's new girlfriend, played by Lindsay Lohan. Age-gap comedy extreme!

And Sarah Jessica Parker on what was surprising about working with Matthew McConaughey: "You know what surprised me is he writes a lot. I didn't know he was a writer. He writes a lot. He really works on the script a lot. He really thinks about it. He breaks it down. I probably would have—if you'd given me truth serum before the rehearsal process—probably thought it comes pretty easy to him, which it does at the same time."

Coming soon: *My Big Fat Racist Wedding.* Starring Matthew McConaughey as a black lawyer betrothed to white girl Mandy Moore. When is he gonna find out that Daddy's in the Klan?

S

"SASSY" SONGS ABOUT BODY PARTS

You're playing with your bits,
I'm playing with my bits,
Ooh baby, I betcha wish you were playing with my bits,
Instead of your bits . . .
My bits, my bits, my bits, my bits, my bits, my bits.

That sort of thing.

ARNOLD SCHWARZENEGGER

- July 3, 2003, pre-campaign appearance in LA: "I told you . . . I'll be baaack!"
- Summer 2003, campaign trail: "By the time I'm through with this whole thing, I will not be known as The Terminator . . . I will be known as The Collectinator!"
- September 14, 2003: "Davis and Bustamante . . . have terminated jobs. They have terminated growth. They have terminated dreams. It is time to terminate them!"
- September 17, 2003: "I know that on October 7, we will recall Gray Davis and say, '*Hasta la vista,* baby!' "

- September 24, 2003, during televised campaign debate to opponent Arianna Huffington: "I just realized that I have a perfect part for you in *Terminator Four*!"
- October 2, 2003: "When I get to Sacramento, I will immediately destroy the car tax. *Hasta la vista,* baby! To the car tax!"
- August 31, 2004, Republican National Convention: "One of my movies was called *True Lies*! It's what the Democrats should have called their convention!"
- August 31, 2004, Republican National Convention: "In one of the military hospitals I visited, I met a young guy who was in bad shape! He'd lost a leg, had a hole in his stomach—his shoulder had been shot through . . . Do you know what he said to me? . . . He grinned at me and said, 'Arnold . . . I'll be back!' "

Did you see what he did there?

SELF-EXAMINATION COLUMNS

"Hmmm . . . have you noticed that no one eats avocados anymore? Wow, think about it a second—it's true. That's amazing—no one eats avocados anymore! We all decided at exactly the same time. Isn't that weird? Or maybe some people do eat them . . . they are still on sale in most places, after all. Anyway! Do you ever get a funny feeling in your left leg? Do you get that? . . ."

The essential skills of the modern columnist rarely overlap with old-style journalism. No more going outside and meeting people, checking facts, or any of that passé nonsense. And at the same time, no need for a blog's timely commentary. No, just make a big sandwich and start examining your own self. Go deep, because when exploring the self, you simply can't be too self-centered. There's no code of conduct to abuse when it's your own privacy you're invading. That would just be like abusing yourself.

But writers can't just write down whatever flickers across their consciousness. Okay, they can. But they also need a gimmick. One successful figure currently produces a weekly treatise focusing solely on fingers. Going under the title "Can You Digit?," a recent missive went: "Hmmm. That nail needs cutting. Look, this one's growing faster than the one on the other hand. Unless I nibbled that one some time after I last cut them all . . ."

Then there was "Everyone I've Ever Spanked Over." This was followed up with "Everyone I've Never Spanked Over," which was pages of the phone book typed out. That column immediately boosted newsstand sales by an estimated 20,000 a week.

A competing title, inspired by such successes, employed another writer to explore the random sounds he could make with his mouth. Called "Sounding Off," it started: "Clickclickclick. That's nice. Babbety-babbety-babbety-bab. Not so sure about that. We're not getting anywhere here. I know—ratatatatatat! ratatatatatat! ratatatatatatat! Yes, I likes it!"

Of course, nobody has yet to top the grandfather of this art form, Larry King. Though his *USA Today* column ended in 2001—in celebration of his ninety-ninth birthday—his unique, tangential brand of batshit crazy remains the self-examining columnist's brass ring. Each week, King would offer up random superlatives along the lines of, "Had dinner with Ann-Margret last week and let me tell you, she is still beautiful . . . For my money, TV doesn't get better than *Chicago Hope* . . . I'll go out on a limb and say food is delicious!"

SERVING SUGGESTIONS

Have the makers of hummus, say, *ever* received a letter complaining that there was no parsley included inside? "The label clearly depicts a parsley garnish atop the tasty chickpea-based Greek dip. So where the shitting hell is it, you robbing pack of thieving bastards? Is it customary for supermarkets willfully to cheat their customers in this way?"

It seems extremely unlikely. Yet there are always two words found on every scrap of food packaging to guard against such an eventuality: SERVING SUGGESTION. They may be small, but they're always there. Like people expect a jug of ice-cold milk to be included in their cereal packet. Even though that would represent a major spillage hazard—which nobody wants. Or a single cherry tomato in their pot of sour cream and onion dip.

The serving suggestions are not only dumb, they're woefully unoriginal. Good Friends cereal is always—always!—served in a clean white bowl. Why not, just once, show an illustration of the oaty cereal having been dished up into a bowl of another color, or into another kind of receptacle altogether: like lots of tiny walnut shells or a pair of child's rubber boots? Now, *that's* a serving suggestion.

SEX TIPS

Some people are so expert at sex that they become "sexperts." Very much leaders in the field of how to use one's bathing suit areas, these people inhabit a world of nonstop sensual erotica. They really know about genitals.

For any willing recipient of the awesome wisdom of a "sexpert," "sex tips" will inject your sex life with such unbridled naughtiness that any passing Bangkok whore would be moved to widen her overpainted eyelids with fearful fascination. Some of the most common "sex tips" include the following:

- Breathe on each other. As one of you breathes out, the other breathes in, so you inhale each other's breath. Breathing—it rocks!
- Cover each other's legs in sealing wax. Hey, it's not for everyone, but don't knock it till you've tried it. Waxy, isn't it?
- Don't underestimate the erotic potential of the elbow. Find out what you can do with yours and before long your love buddy will be dragging you upstairs as soon as you walk in the door.
- Lather up each other's pubic regions with shampoo and make amusing shapes. Laughter is a great way of creating a sexy atmosphere!?!?
- Stuff each other's mouths full of cheese—then lick each other all over. You'll be amazed at the new sensations you both experience.
- You'd be amazed how talking can get your partner feeling horny. Try reading aloud favorite passages from *The Aeneid*. Trust us . . . phew!
- During penetration, why don't you both imagine you are soaring through the clouds on the wings of a giant swan? If either one of you can perform a convincing swan's call, so much the better!

- Oh . . . just, you know, new positions and that. Put your legs in funny places, that sort of thing.

SHOPPED-UP GAS STATIONS

It's like pulling off the freeway for a wee-wee and ending up in one of those airport departure lounges that are one huge duty-free shop so you are fine if your needs are served by perfume, Scotch, and chocolate truffles. But if you are after a bread-based snack, you've got to join a line for the next hour or so to be awarded a stale croissant.

Okay, at Kwik Trip you can buy a bread-based snack at a shop. Or was that Quick Trip? Or Quick Stop? Perhaps Zip Mart? Sprint Mart? Kwik-I-Mart? On-the-Go? Suck & Go? But definitely not a Wawa. All these awful names designed to evoke images of choking down chips and a giant soda while speeding into traffic leaves one wishing for a nice, simple 7-Eleven. Not that anybody knows what "7-Eleven" actually means. Maybe the franchise was started by a Borg named Seven of Eleven.

People actually have to squeeze around each other to avoid the massive piles of water guns, remote-control cars, travel mugs, monster trucks, Wiffle ball kits, watch stands, remote-control dinosaurs, ED-209s, vast selections of doughnuts and popcorn (to keep things calm and puke-free on the backseat). It's like a shop-shit warehouse sale. With the added bonus of a slightly psychotic guy from the AA blocking your entry to the toilet until you make a purchase. Sure, you say you will after you pee, but he knows you're lying. But for him, short of hurting you—which, believe me, he has considered—there's not much he can do about it. His life is a long series of disappointments, adrift in a sea of shop shit.

I'm wiped already—that's why I pulled up in the first place—so I'm not really going to feel utterly refreshed by a veritable shitstorm of shop shit. Honestly, these shitty shopped-up shitholes full of shit shop shit really should just shut up shop and shit off.

SHOPPING CENTERS, NAMES OF

Going to a shopping center is one of the single most painful things known to the sentient human. Calling the place Lakeside or Bluewater will not change that. It is not like being beside a lake. It is like being in hell. There is only one exception to this shopping center name rule and that is Crossroads Bellevue—it's in Bellevue and it makes us feel so psychotically aggrieved that we storm out into the streets, so at least it's factual.

"SIR"/"MADAM"

We supposedly inhabit an infinitely less deferential world, one where priests and judges are not gods to whom we must offer unquestioning obedience but are human, just like the rest of us, only with silly uniforms and more money. Rather than referring to politicians as "Mr. Giuliani" or "Mrs. Clinton," people say things like "dickhead" or "you know, the smarmy bald one." Given this, it's surprising how often you can find yourself, a lowly commoner, being called "sir" or "madam" like you're the ambassador to India ordering high tea at the Ritz. Even though you're just in Blockbuster renting a video. And one of the *Police Academy* series at that.

If you were to purchase some pants, say, and were to approach the earnest clerk behind the register, you can surely pretty much consider each other equals; you could even exchange friendly pleasantries. But not when he calls you "sir" like a scurvy-suffering rat-catcher addressing a dark-clad knight who's holding a broadsword to his skull.

But being a servile service-culture square-bear really doesn't get you anywhere. Unfair though it may seem, when you call me "sir," I am infinitely more inclined to call you "suckass." In reality, the only reason to call someone "sir" is if he could cause permanent damage to your genitals if you didn't. Otherwise, don't bother.

SIX-PACK SECRETS

Six-packs sex you up. That's a fact. According to *Men's Fitness,* "Abdominals are the Top Trump trophy muscles and the ones that drive women wild . . . the abs may have come to symbolize masculinity." Having phenomenal abdominals will "improve your sex appeal and help you achieve your goals" (although the "other goals" men might have besides having sex remain undisclosed). This is why, at some point or other, all men must uncover the secret of the six-pack.

So how does one go about acquiring these bristling sex muscles of sex? As previously explained, it's a secret. You can "crunch" until you're blue in the face, but if you skip the secret stuff, the stuff known only to the chosen few, you are but a modern-day Sisyphus, forever pushing that boulder toward the unattainable peak.

Luckily, some secrets are too much to bear alone, so certain masters of the field have elected to pass on their six-pack lore to the chosen few. There are books with titles like *The Abs Diet: The Six-Week Plan to Flatten Your Stomach and Keep You*

Lean for Life by David Zinczenko and Ted Spiker.* And fitness magazines offering "From Fat to Flat—In Six Weeks!," "Get Hard Abs," or "Abs: Don't Think You Don't Want Them 'Cos You Do Really, Deep Down, Even if You Say You Don't, You Do Really . . ."

"SMART CASUAL"

Workplace clothing policy devised by the Devil, which decrees that suits are too smart and jeans are too casual. So what does that leave in the middle? Fucking chinos.

"SOLD" SIGNS

The property is no longer for sale. This is surely the point at which to take down all those big, fuck-off, multicolored signs outside it. Not put up a new one.

Want to buy this house? Tough shit, you can't. It's not for sale. You should have been here last week. Go and buy another house. 'Cos you ain't buying this one. Want it? I bet you do. But you can't have it.

---

*Other titles include *My Abs Are OK, Your Abs Are OK* by Vince Grundtzenecker. There's also *Make Every Day an Abs Day* by Bunt Masterson. Another alternative is *Abs: The Cosa Nostra Way* by Nico The Chip. Finally, there's *Neat Abs for Invading and Mating Good* by Clay Harbourmouth.

SOUNDTRACK ALBUMS FROM SHIT FILMS WITH SHIT SOUNDTRACKS

Who—*who?*—emerges blinking into the foyer, dusting off a confetti of fumbled popcorn and Milk Duds, after sitting through, say, "Can Pierce Brosnan's master thief resist one last big score with tough cop Woody Harrelson on his tail?" crappy adventure flick *After the Sunset* and thinks: *Hey—great film, must get the soundtrack*?

"Music from and inspired by . . ." That's "inspired" in the financial sense rather than in the actually-having-seen-the-film sense.

When creating his twenty-something mope-fest *Garden State,* Zach Braff seems to have spent more time adding up potential soundtrack sales than writing the script. Mildly successful and mildly handsome actor Braff mopes through his hometown until a quirky meeting with a quirky girl makes him quirkily mope mildly less. Plot-wise, a few seconds would have done—but how then could one crowbar in all of The Shins' first album? What's the Story? We can't remember—there's just this schmuck moping all the time.

Even good films generally have no necessity for a soundtrack release. Who cheers themselves up by listening to the available-at-all-good-record-stores soundtrack to *The Elephant Man*?

Are there really roommates and couples, staring down the end of another evening's TV brain death, saying to each other: "Let's make a night of it. I'll run out to Trader Joe's and get some Two Buck Chuck—you slap on the soundtrack to *Must Love Dogs*."

Or: "Which track from mentalist-insomniac-psycho-factory-worker thriller *The Machinist* do you like best? I really like 'Miserable Life,' but I *love* 'Trevor in Jail.'" "They're both great, but on balance I definitely prefer 'Where Is My Waitress?'" "Yes! The posing of the question, the lack of resolution—it's quite, quite beautiful. Do any of us know the whereabouts of our waitress, really? That's what he's saying. Where is *your* waitress? Where is *my* waitress?"

TV's at it, too, with CD spin-offs from *Grey's Anatomy, CSI, 24,* and *CSI: Miami.* "That quite good drama of Florida-based forensic work certainly enlivened our Monday-evening viewing—let's get the background music from the bits when they were walking down corridors." "Cool. We could walk down our hall."

Even video games have soundtrack albums now—the various volumes of *Grand Theft Auto* have their own section in music stores. "Do you know, later, I think I might pimp some women for a bit and then crash my car." "Awesome. You'll be wanting to put this on then." "Rock on. You motherfucker."

As a general rule, if it's not a musical, it probably doesn't need a soundtrack album. Actually, that holds for most musicals, too. Particularly *Chicago.*

SPAM PORN

"TODAY IS JIZZ DAY!" . . . Is it? Is it really?

SPOTTED!

Someone. Somewhere. Out. Doing stuff. Thanks for that.

STORES THAT PLAY SHIT MUSIC AT EARSPLITTING VOLUME

That's quite a nice shirt, I think I'll pop in there and try—oh, fuck, no I won't, they're playing Nelly Furtado at 12 trillion decibels. Jesus, one of them's even dancing.

STRESS BUSTING, THE PHRASE

It's interesting that, in this day and age, you are even obliged to try to reduce your stress in an aggressive way.

Bust that stress! Get it down on the floor and really stick one on it! Faster! Really fuck it over! You're not good enough! You're not good enough! There isn't time! There isn't time!

STUPID ARGUMENTS FOR BEING PAID TOO MUCH FOR BEING ON TV

After signing John Madden in 2006 to an undisclosed many-millions-of-dollars-a-year contract to cover the NFL, NBC's Dick Ebersol justified the deal by exclaiming, "John Madden is the best analyst in the history of the National Football League and, in my opinion, the best analyst of any kind in sports television history." Okay, possibly. But what he's doing still basically amounts to "watching football," right? Your dad rambles about franchise histories and makes predictions every Sunday, too, only instead of getting filthy rich from it, he loses money by paying for his own beer and chips.

News anchors argue that wheelbarrows are required to pay them because reading the news is "very difficult." Now, we seem to manage it fairly well when we read the paper. We'd go as far as to call it "easy."

The worst lame excuses for minting it for doing nothing are from people on breakfast radio/TV, who always use the argument "We get up really early." This is the reason that they are the third highest-paid occupational group, just behind coffee shop employees and paper boys.

SUMMER BODIES

"Beach panic! Beach panic! Beach panic!"

Summer used to be a time to relax. To feel mellow and laid-back, even. Enjoy a bit of sunshine. Beaches were often seen as the ideal places on which to enact such soothing operations. "Life's a beach," as the saying used to go. But now beaches are places of ungovernable paranoia, as young women are commanded to have "summer bodies for the beach."

You've got to get your body ready for summer. Don't, for fuck's sake, leave it to its own devices. That way lies ruin and derision. Which means, according to the women's magazines, getting into training in the middle of winter. Of course, tans tend to be at their best in autumn, when people start covering up. It's a fundamental flaw in this whole "seasons" thing that we are now thankfully doing our level best to eradicate. By introducing artificial tans that make people look like they have covered themselves in caramel.

And it's not just tans, but having a toned belly, non-nasty toenails, exfoliation, et cetera. This whole getting-ready-for-summer is a fucking nightmare. But it's all-important if you are not going to end the summer sad and lonely, with nothing to look forward to but winter and maybe autumn.

SUPERMARKET FLOWERS

It's a hopeless and forlorn sort of concept, even before you consider their pre-supermarket life cycle: farmed in Colombia by sweated labor, backs to the sun and faces to the earth, wages—topped up with all the free toxic chemicals you can inhale—as pitiful as the blooms; all those wasted, wasted air miles to get them here. That's an oppressive enough litany for coal or iron ore, but for a flower?

Simply of itself, it's quite melancholic: supermarket flowers. In fact, we're surprised somebody hasn't written a sad song incorporating the gift of supermarket flowers as the potent signifier of an empty, artificial relationship. It could be called "Supermarket Flowers."

If anyone now writes one, there'll be no legal comeback from us. It's the sadness we can't bear. That's all.

SURPRISE VISITS TO IRAQ

You would think Prime Minister Nouri al-Maliki might not be in need of any more surprises, what with trying to govern Iraq and all. But in June 2006, George Bush met al-Maliki during a trip to Baghdad that had been kept secret from everyone, including al-Maliki. Visiting the U.S. embassy for a video teleconference with Bush, he instead found himself being greeted by the leader of the free world in person. Surprise!

In photographs, al-Maliki was squirming like someone forced to shake hands with the man now sleeping with his wife. This ambush, after all, proved that Bush needed no permission to enter his country—why, it's practically America! A thought bubble above al-Maliki's head might have said: "I wonder how you would take it if I entered your country unannounced. Would you freak? Oh, I rather think you would. I've got popularity issues enough here, without this doofus turning up."

The Iraqis have probably learned by now to keep the snack cupboard well stocked, given the regularity of surprise visits from Western politicians. If it's not Bush, it's Condoleezza Rice or Dick Cheney or John McCain or some other representative of the forces that aren't trying all that hard not to look like an occupation. Maybe after one too many of these visits, they will blow a fuse and burst: "Look, why don't you just do it? If you like it here so much. You try running it. No? Really? Why not? You want to go home? Oh, really . . ."

Following the Bush visit, the Americans would soon surprise al-Maliki again. After the massacre at Haditha, which allegedly saw U.S. Marines responding to a casualty by killing twenty-four innocent civilians in cold blood, al-Maliki called the incident a "horrible crime," adding that the occupying forces often showed "no respect for citizens, smashing civilian cars and killing on a suspicion or a hunch." The U.S. response? White House Press Secretary Tony Snow said al-Maliki had been "misquoted." The hapless prime minister must have been awestruck. He thought he had said something, but he hadn't! Those crazy guys . . .

But his own government also has a couple of surprises in its arsenal: tens of thousands arrested with only 1.5% convicted of any crime; Finance Minister Bayan Jabr's alleged links to Shi'a death squads (taking the whole Iron Chancellor thing a shade too far). Other occupation shockers: rising deaths from malnutrition and preventable diseases. Electricity and water supplies worse than before the invasion. Half the workforce unemployed with many gaining their sole source of income from selling U.S. Army base junk on the streets (which is a metaphor but also real—inspired!) . . . All things considered, the last thing on the average Iraqi's shopping list is "more surprises."

Perhaps the ultimate punch line to all this: Amid the notable non-rebuilding of the vast majority of Iraq, work on the new U.S. embassy is go, go, go! Building at the 104-acre complex on the banks of the Tigris (prime real estate many believe the United States never paid for), known locally as "George W's palace" (features: the biggest swimming pool in Iraq, a state-of-the-art gym, cinema, numerous U.S. food-chain outlets), is officially a secret, but cranes filling the skyline give the game away. It's like, you know, the Iraq War was this massive folly, and here's an actual massive folly! (It's a metaphor but it's also real—again.)

Or maybe it will be put to good use, as George W's palace! Seriously, maybe as a last surprise for the Iraqi populace, on his retirement from the presidency he will go and live among the people he has liberated from tyranny. Maybe between eating at the massive Pizza Hut and swimming in the biggest swimming pool in Iraq, he could go and stand next to the struggling Iraqi government as they try to quell the civil war, winking at them.

T

TELEVISION ON MOBILE PHONES

Far too small.

TENNIS PARENTS

Human fetuses can't play tennis (not even if it's twins: where would they get the racquets from?). So parents who decide their unborn child is going to be a tennis star have to be some kind of freaky freaking freak-nutter freaking freaks.

Richard Williams, father of Venus and Serena, consulted psychiatrists about the best way to bring up children destined for sporting stardom. Possibly quite sensible, given their early promise on the tennis court. Except he did it before they were born. Freaky freaking freak-nutter freaking freak.

Melanie Molitor, mother of Martina Hingis, was so determined her unborn child would be a tennis star that she named her after Martina Navratilova. Still, that's better than calling her Boris. Or Goran. Or Pat Cash (Pat Cash Hingis—that's a shit name). Anyway, aged four, Martina was playing in tennis tournaments—as opposed to, say, with LEGOs.

So keen was Damir Dokic—father of Jelena—on dominating his daughter that he has found it very hard to let go. The right-wing nationalist Serbian ex-boxer made a name for himself by getting expelled from matches for hurling Serbian abuse at officials (which puts your own dad's "embarrassing" sweater in perspective). Perhaps wisely, his daughter expressed her gratitude by dumping him as manager and moving to a different country. He responded: "She left us. We don't need her . . . She did things that she was not supposed to."

And why tennis, anyway, which is shit? Why not mold your children to do something useful—like perfecting nuclear fusion, or playing the drums like Animal out of the Muppets? And those freaks who "hothouse" their kids into genius mathematicians are no better. Hothouses are for growing tomatoes in. Is that what you want your child to be: a tomato? Freaky freaking freak-nutter freaking freaks.

We believe the children are the future. Teach them well and let them lead the way; show them all the beauty they possess inside. Let the children's laughter remind us how we used to be. Actually, come to think of it, that's not us—that's Whitney Houston. Same difference.

TESTING CHILDREN TO MAKE THEM CLEVER

Tests used to be a way of seeing whether children were learning stuff rather than, say, just picking their noses and flicking it. Nowadays, children learn stuff so they can pass tests, so everyone can see that they are good at passing tests. If the first is the horse pulling the cart, the second is more like the cart pulling the horse and then making it take a test.

Children are now made to take tests on the morning they enter school. Then, in the afternoon, they are made to take a test on what they have learned from that morning's test. Get that sandbox out of here! What do you think this is: fun? Or maybe we could test them on their sandbox abilities . . .

It's a testing situation. One that has intriguing ramifications for the nation's psyche. Critics of this education system point out that this cram-based learning fails to instill in children any "reading stamina" for whole books. Reading a book from cover to cover? No chance. Not even a short one. (They were fine with turning over the paper, but . . .)

TICKETING HOTLINES

"The bill for your $25.50 ticket comes to $46.99." "Great."

TOAST, OVERPRICED

There's a lot of overpriced toast out there. Watch out.

TOY CARS

Are aspirational these days. They're all big Mercedes and Audi TTs. Visit any toy shop looking to gift up a little person and you'll find all the household names in the die-cast mini motor universe—Matchbox, Siku, Hot Wheels—wholly obsessed with premium automobiles.

There's seemingly a ban on ordinary cars—the sort most people drive, the sort most children might ever see. No Civics or Yarises or Focuses or Kias—or even any Saabs or Lexi (that's the plural of Lexus, by the way). Toyota Prius? Not on your happy ass. The message: "Hey, I know you think he's good, but sorry, kid, your dad's a loser."

You'll be falling over huge delivery trucks branded with DHL or UPS logos, but searching high and low for an ambulance. You can still get fire engines—except they have to be either 40 feet long with 18 retractable ladders and called Flame Tamer, or have TURBO written down the side.

What next? Conservatories for dollhouses? Marbles made out of actual marble? My Little Gated Community? Doctors and Nurses could become Senior HMO Manager and Drug Company Rep. Simon Says: "Swarovski Rocks!"

TRAILERS FOR PROGRAMS THAT ARE ON TV NOW

An ad for a program advertising the fact that said program is on "next" or even "now"—that is, as soon as this trailer and the announcer announcing that the program is starting get out of the way, the program will start.

Surely trailers should trail programs that will be on in the future, rather than those that are on in the present. We don't think of that as a complicated point.

TRENDS IN INTERIOR DESIGN

Interiors magazines tell you that September is the month to:

- Decorate the walls with bird motifs.
- Discover the beauty of stained glass.
- Use summer's harvest produce to make jellies and chutneys.

No, it's not. It's the month to go to work/school/college, eat toast, drink too much, forget to do stuff, and watch some TV. Rather like October. And November.

What do you mean you haven't repainted the whole house yet this week? Didn't you know that "warm, vibrant, and lively, orange is set to become next season's hottest color"? Meaning that having a stylish house actually means having an orange house.

Until, that is, six months down the line when—with your house barely free of the smell of orange paint—the same homes mag wags its shitty little finger at you and says, "Sophisticated, mellow, and organic, sage green is set to become next season's hottest color."

What shall I do with my orange carpet? Burn the bastard in the street as punishment for it not being sage? My house looks like a fucking Tang commercial.

"New looks for table linen"? Shove them up your ass.

DONALD TRUMP

The Apprentice supremo Donald Trump—and this is true—claims he grows those amazing trademark eyebrows *on purpose*. They are alpha-male stag antlers designed to intimidate opponents in negotiations. Okay, but what about the stupid hair?

Big Don has a holiday Web site called—and this is equally true—www.gotrump.com. He also has a property Web site called www.pumptrump.org. Okay, he hasn't. But GoTrump is real. In fact, we'd highly recommend listening to Trump's welcome speech on the home page, where he shouts at you like an evangelical car salesman pumped up on sales after a sales seminar at a power-selling away-day: "There's nobody better—there's nobody even close."

Advanced megalomania—that definitely puts us in the holiday mood. Although we would be even more enthusiastic if they had animated the eyebrows.

T-SHIRTS, INSANELY EXPENSIVE

The turnover for T-shirts in the U.S. economy is now greater than for all other commodities combined—including food and oil. This is due to the strategy of charging fuckloads of money for them, even though, at the end of the day, they're only T-shirts that cost approximately jack squat to produce.

Not long ago, one could reasonably be expected to be an outcast from society for wearing a JOURNEY T-shirt. Not anymore, though—not now that they cost $70. What about a fake-aged AC/DC T-shirt—a brand-new T-shirt that looks like a faded 1980s tour T-shirt? A mere $69. Or maybe a fake-aged THE FINAL COUNTDOWN BY EUROPE T-shirt—a tad more expensive at $75 (because it's about 8.7% more ironic).

Some of these desirable items are produced by a company called, ahem, Buddhist Punk. An iron law of insanely expensive T-shirt making states that your company must have a silly name—a bit, you know, funky. (See ***Funky,* the Word, as Applied to Anything Except a Musical Genre**.) Top marks here must go to the company Maharishi. Christ, if you're chump enough to give them seventy bucks, you can't say they weren't advertising the fact they could see you coming. You couldn't give a much bigger clue short of calling your company Faker. Or Snake-Oil. Or Skank.

Oh, but they've probably been also "customized" (someone

has added a bad print of Hong Kong Phooey or Al Pacino as Scarface). Or even "deconstructed"—that is, with seams on the outside, or bits of material added to, you know, consider the workings of your T-shirt and unpack its very, erm, T-shirt-ness. "Deconstructed" T-shirts are the very apex of T-shirt design and are always—always—the work of major designers. M-A-J-O-R. People who don't just design T-shirts but also do, you know, trousers, maybe even coats.

Please understand that these T-shirts are very expensive—anywhere up to $200—because it takes a major talent to do this and only a major talent. Or a monkey. For fuck's sake.

TV BULLIES

Television is only entertaining when we're watching someone else's lifestyle being torn to shreds with the brutal, yet oddly humane, efficiency of Orwell's chief interrogator O'Brien.

The main draw of TV's top-rated show, *American Idol,* is watching judge Simon Cowell tear the contestants a new asshole when their Bryan Adams cover doesn't live up to Cowell's high standards. Sounding like a less friendly version of Waldorf or Statler from the Muppets, every week he drops cruel bon mots like, "If you would be singing like this two thousand years ago, people would have stoned you." And all of that is still nicer than his weekly gay bashing of possibly-not-gay Ryan Seacrest.

On *America's Next Top Model,* not only must contestants conquer, er, top modeling challenges (Like walking while wearing clothes? Doing coke? Dating Rod Stewart?), but they must also survive the verbal assaults of lunatic Tyra Banks. She once brought a challenger who disappointed her to tears by screaming, "Be quiet, Tiffany! Be quiet! Stop it! I have never in my life yelled at a girl like this." Yes, this is reality TV, but must that reality sound so much like an abusive marriage?

Supernanny Jo Frost has got so carried away with the Nietzschean implications of her calling that she dresses up like a Nazi dominatrix. It's a potent sight, but what kind of message does it send out to the kiddies? Maybe FX should show *Supernanny Plus* in which she administers some light, after-hours whipping to a daddy who can't control his offspring.

What we need now is a single program combining all the elements of ritual humiliation called *How Do You Like Having Your Psyche Rearranged, You Fuck?* An English headmaster could visit the homes of ordinary citizens and shout: "Your hair is crap. Your house is puke. Your clothes are trash. Your kids are shit. You smell appalling. And I'm afraid, my dear, that you don't seem to know the first thing about making love. Here's a loaded pistol. Do the decent thing, there's a good soldier."

U

ÜBER, THE PREFIX

As in *übertrendy, über-cool, über-stylish,* and, of course, *über-gruppenführer.* The question we must always ask ourselves before embarking on any leisure activity is: *Will this put me in a higher social position than my contemporaries?* Otherwise, what's the point? After all, it's not a game.

These days, you can read an überhip novel surrounded by übercool kids in an überflash drinking environment. You can mix it on the high-end ski slopes with the überstylish powder hounds. Or dine at New York's übertrendy Tenjune restaurant, spending a hundred bucks a head (which is in no way überpriced). Or you can leave cattle class and use private hospitals to become an überconsumer.

Surprisingly often, cutting an überdash means flashing some übercash. And, logically, if one is not an über then one is, dismally, an unter. You never pay a hundred bucks a head for your dinner? That's sad. It's probably not your fault, but you really do deserve to be enslaved. Are there any railways that still need building?

Stratifying humans into unders and overs seems a satisfyingly simple way of dividing society. And don't we all like simple überideas?

UNDERSTANDING BUSINESS

Everyone thinks we should "understand business." We have no business not understanding business. We should very much make it our business. To understand business. Personally, we make it our business scrupulously to avoid business. But that's our business.

One man out to make you—YES YOU!!!—understand business is Jim Cramer, host of CNBC's *Mad Money*. Well, we think he wants to help us make money. He opens every episode by shouting "Let's try to make some money!" But as we wrote, he does SHOUT THIS VERY LOUDLY, which is also how he communicates EVERY OTHER THOUGHT HE HAS!!! So he could also be trying to make us deaf. BOOO YAAA!!!

Cramer made between $50 and $100 million as a hedge-fund manager in the 1990s, so in theory he should understand business. (See **Hedge-Fund Boys**.) And yet, according to many other Wall Street wizards, he's a crock. Alan Abelson of *Barron's* slammed Cramer in a 2004 column, showcasing how one batch of the *Mad Money* man's stock picks tanked by an average of 90%.

There was also a Web site run by Cramer critics called CramerWatch.org, where not only did they track the failure of many of Mr. Cramer's stock picks, but they also offered up their own picks by Leonard the Wonder Monkey. Who was a simian. And often just as accurate at picking stocks to invest in.

One thing we have learned about business came from

watching *The Apprentice,* and that is that even people who are really into business don't understand it. Most of the contestants haven't got a fucking clue. About anything. Set them a simple task like "go and buy these items for the cheapest price" and they will flap around like an elderly person suddenly commanded to drive Formula One. Unless we're missing something and one key business skill involves being fairly average but shouting loudly that you are, in fact, not average. "Average? Me?! Get out of here! I'm the best. I know I'm fucking everything up and no one likes me, but I'm the kind of guy who gets things done and can get on with anybody. Buy stuff, people! Buy stuff!"

UNITED NATIONS, THE

See **Vox, Bono.**

UNNECESSARY DIGITIZATION

In Europe, Virgin's new Pendolino trains have special tiny screens set into the carriage walls just above the windows, telling you whether seats 045 and 046, say, are AVAILABLE or, conversely, NOT AVAILABLE.

The screens are tiny. The carriage lights are set into the wall just above them—and thus shine directly over the faint LED lettering, which sits on/merges into a light gray-green background. Even with 20/20 vision, you have to squint to read them, leaning in right over the top of the double seat.

So maybe a more efficient, faster, easier method of discerning whether a seat is AVAILABLE or NOT AVAILABLE would be to look at the seat and decide whether there is someone sitting in it.

(Or, conversely, NOT SITTING IN IT.) Old-fashioned, perhaps, but less likely to require the utilization of binoculars.

Digital scales, meanwhile: The only people who need those are drug dealers.

UNNECESSARY GREETING CARDS

"For my wife . . . On Mother's Day." Such messages are presumably intended to carry the subtext: "For my wife on Mother's Day, because, as you know, I tend to think of you as my mother." Or maybe: "Because I love you in much the same way as I love my mother." In either case, don't expect a nice dinner.

We didn't realize Mother's Day meant giving cards to every woman in our acquaintance. How about: "For my childless female friend, the one without kids, on Mother's Day, because you have the potential to be a mother—which is a great and beautiful thing. (Even though you do, as we think we have discussed before, get a bit irritating when you've had too much to drink.)"

"Congratulations on your divorce." Presumably comes with the message: "Roses are red/Violets are blue/You didn't get the house/But you did get the canoe . . ."

Not forgetting:

"Congratulations on your teeth whitening."

"Happy Prom, princess."

And, of course: "Commiserations on the death of the life partner you stole from me. Rot in hell, you fuck."

UNOFFICIAL "SPONSORS" OF SPORTING EVENTS

For shame! Apparently there are companies out there that want the honor of sponsoring the Super Bowl or World Series without the glory of paying nearly $3 million per spot. So marketers for these products roll out campaigns aimed to capitalize on these sporting events . . . without specifically mentioning the event.

Since Coors and Anheuser-Busch already had the exclusive NFL contracts, Miller created its own Super Bowl tie-in in 2007 by running a contest offering a visit from NFL Hall of Famer Eric Dickerson to the winner's house for the "Feb. 5 game." Why, let me check my calendar and see who's playing on the fifth . . . oh, look, it's Super Bowl Sunday! What a coincidence!

ConAgra Foods, Inc.—home to B-level food brands like Hunt's Ketchup, Swiss Miss hot chocolate, and Jiffy Pop popcorn—took a B-level approach to NFL's big game also, by hiring former pro/current commentator Boomer Esiason to hawk its food in ads that happen to run—wait for it again—during the "Feb. 5th game." Integrated marketing manager Corey Saenz bragged about the scam to *USA Today,* saying, "What's nice about Boomer is that he gives us NFL credibility without tying into the NFL per se."

Fair or unfair, at least second-rate beer and hot dogs deserve to be sold to football fans. They are the target demo. But toilet paper? Yes, says Scott bath tissue, which hired former Bears coach Mike Ditka to urge consumers to cut the danger of clogs during the "Big Game's" halftime bathroom rush by using its easily dissolvable toilet paper. Well played, shit paper. Well played.

The key to these unofficial sponsors' success: euphemisms. None of them said the words *Super* and *Bowl* in the same thirty seconds. That was the fatal flaw in Bowl-O-Rama's decision to promote its new Super Bumper Lanes during the "Big Game." Those bowling lanes now belong to the NFL's lawyers.

U.S. VERSIONS OF UK REALITY SHOWS

Dancing on Ice becomes *Skating with Celebrities,* what with the original being too hard to understand.

V

"VARIOUS THINGS TO DO BEFORE YOU DIE" LISTS

Whole series of listy travel books convey the message: "Don't die before seeing Borneo. For then, you will not have lived."

Or even the Finger Lakes! Look, we've seen the Finger Lakes, and we can honestly say we could have easily lived without seeing them. They were okay but, well, we haven't been back—which kind of says it all.

"Unforgettable Things to Do Before You Die"? Although there is not much point doing something "unforgettable" just "before you die" because you won't actually have too much opportunity to forget it. Maybe a subtitle should point out that: "You Might Want to Do Them Awhile Before You Die, Otherwise Their Unforgettable Nature Might Be Somewhat Wasted on You."

Of course, another way of saying "Things to Do Before You Die" is "Things to Do While You're Still Alive," which rather goes without saying, unless we are to assume that there are loads more boxes to tick off of "Things to Do After We Have Stopped Living." The primary thing about these kinds of lists is . . . look, it's not going to happen. And if it did happen, you would quite clearly, and quite tragically, have set about methodically experiencing life with the spontaneous zeal of a solicitor's desk clerk catching up on invoices, which rather defeats the life-seizing object you are seeking to convey.

I don't want to die.

VILLAGE PEOPLE, THE, NOT BEING GAY

In 2005, the Village People's lawyer protested that the whole gay thing surrounding the group was a travesty of the truth. The lawyer had decided the members needed a more "mainstream" image and barred inclusion of their songs in an upcoming gay rights documentary.

This is a bit rich, seeing as their hits included "YMCA," which said: "Get some man-love at the YMCA." And "In the Navy," which exhorted listeners to: "Get some man-love in the navy."

A little-known fact is that, after their first flush of success, the boyz tried to update their sound. The 1981 album *Renaissance* (and this is 100% true) saw them morph into a hideous electro-pop outfit, styled as New Romantics. We hesitate to suggest you look up the pictures on the Internet, so just try to imagine, instead of the Cop, the Indian, or the Construction Worker, a black Steve Strange with a mustache-goatee combo standing with his legs apart, crotch thrust forward, like . . . well, like a member of the Village People.

And is this lawyer also maintaining that the New Romantic Village People weren't gay?

VOLUME OF TV ADS

Too loud.

VOX, BONO

In the run-up to Live 8, Bono explained to the *Evening Standard* the full burden of his responsibilities: "I represent a lot of people [in Africa] who have no voice at all . . . They haven't asked me to represent them. It's cheeky but I hope they're glad I do."

Cheeky? Not a bit of it!

Previously, during the fiftieth-anniversary celebrations of the United Nations, he explained exactly why the institution was so important: "[I] live off some of the statistics provided by [the UN]—it gives [me] the facts so that when I rant I have something to go on. Without Kofi Annan saying, 'You have an open door at any time, Bono,' I wouldn't have the same intelligence. You need to know what's happening on the ground."

People often wonder what the UN is for. It is, we now discover, essentially a fact-finding service for Bono, the world's most important man, who has come here to save us, each and every one of us.

Bono is all around. Tonight: Thank God it's him, instead of you.

W

WAITS ON EVEREST

Have you seen the lines? Fucking atrocious. Don't know why they don't hire more staff.

The fact that Mount Everest is "really high" need no longer be a barrier to having a fun day out for all the family. Like Legoland, but with less oxygen.

Everyone's been up there, including the first double amputee and the first *Playboy* cover model. The ascent is now littered with abandoned oxygen bottles, soft-drink cans, and shredded tents. There are piles of human excrement; toilet paper is referred to locally as "white man's prayer flags."

Oh, and corpses. One in twenty people who go up don't come back. That's not because they like it so much that they decide to stay. At the time of this writing, 203 people have been killed on Everest since records began in 1922—11 of them in April and May 2006 alone.

Strangely, the waiting lines for Everest do not appear to make it completely safe. In fact, they might help foster the illusion that climbing the world's highest mountain is a breeze. One experienced mountaineer recently told Radio 4's *You and Yours:* "I was on the North Camp with people who had not worn crampons before." Some people thought Sherpas were a type of van.

Others might be deluded that someone will help them to safety if something goes wrong. This is not necessarily true. When David Sharp had to stop after he became ill on his way down from the summit in May 2006, it has been estimated that as many as forty climbers passed by on their way up the mountain. A few gave Sharp oxygen or supplies, but none attempted to rescue him. He died.

In 1996, two Japanese climbers came upon a frostbitten but still conscious Indian climber slumped in the snow. Although the Japanese were carrying food and oxygen, they ignored him. Higher up, they passed two more stricken Indian climbers, one conscious and kneeling in the snow. Again, they passed by. One explained: "Above 26,000 feet is not a place where people can afford morality."

How's that, then? You're just on your holidays. You're not the first ones to do it. Although the late Edmund Hillary said: "On my expedition, there was no way you'd have left a man under a rock to die."

When Hillary died in early 2008, much was made in obituaries of his noble refusal to admit that he had actually beaten his Sherpa companion Tenzing to the summit—until, that is, after Tenzing had died. Nobody admitted the possibility that maybe he wasn't the first after all, but just waited until his old mate had croaked to claim he was. We're not saying that this happened, only that it could have. The sly old mountain goat.

WASHED AND READY-TO-EAT VEGETABLES

A fantastic way for supermarkets to turn a bag of carrots at 79 cents per pound into a bag of scrubbed carrot batons at $3 per pound.

Batons? Don't make us laugh. You couldn't run a relay race using anything of that size. You'd be almost certain to drop it during the changeover.

WATER

If you are still drinking ordinary water, you must be some kind of freaking loser. We wouldn't drink ordinary water—bottled or tap—if you paid us, which, apart from anything else, would be quite a weird thing to do on your part. We only drink "ultra-purified," "restructured" Penta—"the Choice of Champions." Too fucking right it is. This shit is scientific. Consider this blurb from the side of the bottle: "Top athletes use Penta for ultimate performance." Drinking this stuff makes you run faster: *fact.*

"Busy mums and high-flyers use Penta to rise above the daily grind." Anything endorsed by both athletes and moms—well, that's got to be some serious shit. Which it is. Highfliers are usually total shitheads but, hey, they need water, too. And it's reassuring to know that when some fucknuts on Wall Street are bankrupting Guatemala, they're very, very hydrated and are therefore much more likely to piss their pants.

So what's in it? Water! Yes, just freaking water—but more water than in old-fashioned water. That's right, there's more water per centiliter of our water than your Earthling water, you shit-water drinking fool. If you had 500 milliliters of your shitty water, and we had 500 milliliters of Penta, we'd have more water than you. Having trouble getting your brain around that? Try getting "Bio-hydrated": It makes you alert, more intelligent, and (oh yes!) more likely to bang and be banged by fit people.

Not only is Penta "easy to drink" (how difficult can water get—unless it's just been boiled in a kettle? But still, cool), it's also "fast acting." Because old water, while perfectly adequate for the Steam Age, is now just so frigging slow. If you've got broadband but still use taps, you're clearly some kind of chumpy monkey. So get with it, monkey chump.

In fact, the next time your local water authority comes knocking, demanding to know why you haven't paid the bill, tell them to shove their water up their ass, it's shit.

WEATHERPEOPLE'S BABY TALK

The audience for most weather reports consists of particularly wee three-year-olds. This is why, if it's "chilly out and about," the audience needs instructing to "wrap up nice and warm." If the sun's coming out to play, we should all be careful because its rays can be very strong. And if there's rain coming, the forecaster adopts a special pained expression: "Naughty, *naughty* meteorological system!"

Okay, there might be a case for wincing slightly when relaying how another record has just been broken; that, thanks to the wonders of climate change, we have just witnessed the hottest February ever and Vermont is aflame with burning bushes. But no, they get quite jolly over that sort of thing.

"Spits and spots of rain"? Fuck that.

WEB 2.0

Haven't finished reading the first one yet.

WEB PORTALS

Judging by the home pages of AOL, Yahoo!, and MSN, the Internet is just one fucking massive, world-spanning copy of the *New York Post.*

Chirpy presentation; perhaps a bit of news, although not much; asinine lifestyle tips, consumer articles that aren't really; sex tips; astrology (obviously); pictures of what's hot and what's not on the red carpet. Where are the conspiracy theories? The swirly graphics trying to sell you stuff? The good old-fashioned fully nude humping? Now *that's* the Internet. At least you can read the *Post* in the bath.

WEB SITES, SUPERFLUOUS

Surely the correct response to an ad for a new chocolate ice cream is either "That looks quite nice—I might buy some" or "Nope, not for me" or total indifference. Not: "Thank God they've set up a Web site about this ice cream, so I can find out more information before committing myself to such a significant purchase."

At the movies, on TV, and in magazines, ads for, say, new sneakers direct you to a Web site solely dedicated to moving pictures of those selfsame new sneakers—presumably in case you haven't quite grasped the ramifications of the whole "there are some new sneakers on sale" message and need to research the issue further in the comfort of your own home.

Visit any of these sites and your screen will (assuming you've got the right plug-in) explode into a thousand swirling colors. For a brief moment, you'll be dazzled at how your crappy PC can contain such visions of kaleidoscopic wonder. Then you think: *Why? Someone spent ages making that happen. Why?*

WORK EXPERIENCE

Employment arrangement that enables companies to shift their training costs on to middle-class parents.

"WORK HARD/PLAY HARD"

"We need our weekends to get over our weeks and need our weeks to get over our weekends."

So says the modern office worker, whose lifestyle is closely resembling that of Mötley Crüe in their mid-1980s Sunset Strip prime. Rather than, say, a stupendously unquestioning twentysomething couple who frequent a few after-hours bar-clubs following a week spent so far up their boss's ass they could clean the inside of his hat.

The general public is working longer hours, drinking more booze, and drugging more drugs than ever before. We work stupid hours and then relieve the stress by hammering our bodies with toxins, and—unlike, say, a Victorian chimney sweep whacked up on gin—we think this equates to radical high living rather than just alternating between the twin modes of droney worker and droney consumer.

Soon, we will all be obliged to work and play so hard that the two will need to be combined. Young professionals will be standing around in All Bar One of an evening typing up reports on their Palm Pilots while chugging back bottles of absinthe and eating Marlboro Lights. Young workers will conduct presentations from the middle of the dance floor in Area, showing flow charts on a projector normally employed for "psychedelic visuals." Staff appraisals will be carried out in the ladies' toilets while racking out a line on the top of a filthy hand dryer.

The offices, meanwhile, will have bars and cigarette machines and people from the head office hanging around the leather-sofaed chill-out area whispering "powder?" Everyone will be living like Steve Rubell at the height of his pre-bust Studio 54 24-hour fuck-and-coke-athon.

This means that, before long, everyone will eventually crash out, go into rehab, come out, and be played by Mike Myers in the biopic. Which is a worry.

WORLD LEADERS, MESSIANIC

You might have thought that, given the choice between a messianic leader and a nonmessianic leader, most people would realize that the latter was safer by far. Sadly, though, some populations can't resist the lure of leaders with delusionally apocalyptic ideas of saving the world by getting their God on, who think there is a big man up there telling them to bring about a clash of civilizations. Which is a shame.

The buildup of tension between America and Iran has been particularly intriguing in this regard, being a clear stand-off between one person who believes in the coming messiah and another who believes in the coming messiah—albeit, problematically, a different messiah.

The Iranian uranium enrichment program has focused attention like little else on the messianic thoughts of elected president, and world-renowned Holocaust denier, Mahmoud Ahmadinejad.

Just before announcing that Iran had gate-crashed "the nuclear club," he disappeared for several hours to hold a mystic meeting with the Hidden Imam, an arcane figure who has apparently been hiding in "grand occultation" since the tenth century and whom Ahmadinejad believes will soon return to earth to embark upon a climactic face-off with all enemies. The subsequent all-singing, all-dancing show put on by way of celebration was great, a bit like *High School Musical* but with added uranium.

Luckily for everyone, nobody in the "infidel" West would ever dream of getting caught up in anything so dangerous and irrational as a clash of civilizations. Excepting, perhaps, the Bush White House. The born-again President W. has, after all, said that he invaded Muslim countries because his Christian God told him to. How do we know this? Because he carefully explained this to a gathering of Muslim leaders. According to Nabil Shaath, Palestinian foreign minister at the time, at a meeting in 2005: "President Bush said to all of us: 'I am driven with a mission from God. God would tell me, "George go and fight these terrorists in Afghanistan." And I did. And then God would tell me, "George, go and end the tyranny in Iraq." And I did.' " I would like to have seen their faces after that.

Bush actively considered destroying Iran's capabilities with a nuclear bomb—the first used in anger since 1945. According to Seymour Hersh in the *New York Times,* senior military officials tried to remove the nuclear option, as such an insanely inflammatory act might not play well with the world's 1.2 billion Muslims. The White House insisted the option must be retained. Using information from his Pentagon sources, Hersh said of Bush: "It is his mission, his messianic mission if you will, to rid the world of this menace . . . He thinks he's the only one now who will have the courage to do it."

"Courage": Yes, that's definitely what he's got. Responding to this, BBC Middle East correspondent Jeremy Bowen pondered that maybe the situation was not totally as dire as it seemed to be: "Are they telling [Hersh] the truth or is this some kind of disinformation operation?" he wondered. "It could suit the Bush administration for people to believe they are not rational when in fact they are."

It's sort of comforting to know that actions which appear irrational could, in fact, actually hide a deeper rationality. That's much better. And, certainly, these guys are not usually in the habit of taking fairly hairy risks about that kind of thing. Except, perhaps, for the time when the CIA handed instructions to the Iranians about how to build an atomic bomb.

According to *New York Times* reporter James Risen's book *State of War,* in 2000 the CIA began the really quite flaky Operation Merlin, an intriguing experiment aimed at throwing Iran off the scent that involved passing on nuclear secrets—Russian blueprints for a crucial component known as the TBA-480 high-voltage block—but first making them slightly wrong. It had worked with other weapons designs and so, the thinking went, it could also work for nuclear bombs—sending Iranian scientists down a dead end for years. It's like a fun trick, but a fun trick that sort of passes nuclear secrets to Iran.

What could possibly go wrong? Well, what reportedly went wrong was that the CIA's Russian scientist, a defector who lived in the United States, spotted the CIA's intentional flaw and, rather misunderstanding the nature of his mission, added a helpful note tipping the Iranians off to the problem. It was, one could definitely assert, a mistake. But an honest mistake. We've all made them. Although ours don't usually involve passing nuclear secrets to Iran.

WRAPS

A chicken wrap? With a lower half that's basically one massive reef knot of pita dough? That actually admits on the packaging to containing just 20% chicken to 40% wrap? And that's 20% by weight, meaning that—given the way chicken weighs more than wrap—the chicken peeking out of the top is essentially all the chicken anyone is getting in this chicken pita wrap? That is not, in any real sense, a wrap—in the sense of something being wrapped up in wrapping. That's just wrapping with some incidental stuff nearby, as if by coincidence rather than intent.

Healthy Option pita wraps even make big claims to "have less stuff in." Don't fucking boast about it! Why not put a big sticker on saying: NOW CONTAINS *NO* FUCKING STUFF WHATSOEVER!

X

X, THE LETTER, AT THE START OF WORDS WHERE IT ISN'T

I see you, products incorporating *Xtra* or *Xpress*. If you think you're saving letters by dropping the *e*, you're actually using loads more than you need to because it's all a bunch of nonsense. Remember this rule of thumb: If you wouldn't get points for it in Scrabble, it will look retarded as the name of your store.

X&Y

The creation of Coldplay's epochal third album was riven with pain and strife. One version of the album was scrapped completely as the band decided to start again from scratch. During the tortured process, around fifty songs were junked to make way for the final selection.

So, what . . . there were fifty songs not as good as the ones on the final album? Really? What, worse than that first one?

XANAX ADDICTS

What's wrong with Hollywood people these days? Getting addicted to Xanax, Vicodin, Ambien, or other assorted mother's little helps: It's not very James Caan, is it? OxyContin sounds like a zit cream.

Certainly, on one level, an addiction to prescription painkillers does have logic on its side. If taking drugs is a way of killing the pain, then clearly the ultimate painkilling drug would be the painkiller. It's kind of the mother lode. But the outlaw chic that drug use supposedly confers on the user is somewhat diluted by the "prescription" element.

Did Francis Ford Coppola and crew film *Apocalypse Now* on drugs that made your legs wobbly and your speech slow and slurred? They did not. They used high-octane cocaine. These were very much the go-getters of the age. Would they ever have made it up the river pumped up on Xanax? No, they would just have wobbled about in the hotel room for a while. Then they'd have had a bite to eat.

XENU

The Church of Scientology's theory of Xenu, its highest level of wisdom, must be imparted only to those who have ascended to the zenith of human development (that is, people like Tom Cruise). This is because lesser people trying to process the revelations may die; that is actually the stated reason. But we will now reveal to you what OT (Operating Thetan) level Scientologists pay probably hundreds of thousands of dollars and devote many years of effort to learn. Be brave. Gird thyself, or turn away, damn you . . .

Basically, humans are made of clusters of spirits (or "thetans") who were banished to earth some 75 million years ago by an evil galactic warlord named Xenu. Suspecting rebellion due to overpopulation, Xenu—ruler of a galactic confederacy that consisted of 26 stars and 76 planets (including the earth, which was then known as Teegeeack)—duped citizens into attending "income tax inspections," where he drugged them and shipped them off to Teegeeack. They wore clothes "which looked very remarkably like the clothes they wear this very minute" (wrote L. Ron Hubbard), and were shipped in planes that were exact copies of Douglas DC-8s, "except the DC-8 had fans, propellers on it and the space plane didn't."

Through the Scientology process of "auditing," the thetan—who has lived through many past lives and will continue to live beyond the death of the body—can free itself of "engrams" and "implants" (the accumulated crud of ages) and thus recover its native spiritual abilities—gaining control over matter, energy, space, time, thoughts, form, and life. This freed state is called Operating Thetan.

How are you feeling? Dead yet? Do you still want a free stress test?

Scientology claims to be the "study of truth." Which is almost amusing. The church was founded in 1954 by L. Ron Hubbard. Tired of his unsuccessful attempts to be a pulp writer (he had also previously flunked college and was discharged from the U.S. Navy), he told acquaintances: "I'd like to start a religion. That's where the money is"; and "If a man really wants to make a million dollars, he should start a religion." So he started a religion and got rich. The richer the church got, the more Hubbard could deal with his own stress—ultimately de-stressing by cruising around the Mediterranean in his own liner with lots of foxy women in uniforms attending on him.

(Since Hubbard's death in 1986, the church has been run by David Miscavige.)

How did Hubbard discover the "Space Opera" that is the Xenu revelation? The revelation came to him in 1966–67, when he conducted a series of "audits" on himself to unearth what he believed to be his hidden or suppressed memories, using an EMeter (the primitive lie detector used by Scientology in its stress tests/"intensives"). In a letter to his wife of the time, Mary Sue, Hubbard said that to assist his research he was drinking a great deal of rum and taking a cocktail of stimulants and depressants ("I'm drinking lots of rum and popping pinks and grays"). His assistant, Virginia Downsborough, revealed that he "was existing almost totally on a diet of drugs." Well, it was the mid-1960s: Everyone was at it. But you wouldn't let "I Had Too Much to Dream (Last Night)" by the Electric Prunes become the basis for a religion, would you?

The church now claims ten million members in 159 countries and more than six thousand churches, missions, and outreach groups. Volunteers sign contracts donating a "billion years" of labor. Scientology charges for virtually all its services: Intensives, those little chats about your engrams, can, according to Janet Reitman in *Rolling Stone,* "cost anywhere from $750 for introductory sessions to between $8,000 and $9,000 for advanced sessions." Being registered as a religion, of course, means the church is tax-exempt.

Anyone thinking critically within the church is marked down as a Potential Trouble Source. Those trying to leave have to go through a yearlong "route out" process, during which they are put under immense pressure to stay. Critics outside the church have been intimidated with litigation, and also by more direct, old-fashioned methods.

Katie Holmes was, of course, famously told by the church to remain silent while giving birth to Tom Cruise's child (lest the trauma induce engrams in the baby). A spokesperson for the church claimed they actually meant the delivery staff, and Katie could make the occasional noise if she absolutely needed to. Oh, that's okay then. Except that the average woman would probably appreciate a few words of encouragement from delivery staff during labor. It really hurts.

But what do we non-Scientologists—or "common, ordinary, run of the mill, garden-variety humanoid[s]" (Hubbard)—know? Who are we to question the right of people to be blackmailed, brainwashed, and separated from their families while having their heads filled with horseshit about aliens? Each to their own. Or, as Kabbalah-worshipping freak Madonna put it: "If it makes Tom Cruise happy, I don't care if he prays to turtles."

Thus speaks the voice of reason.

Y

YOUTUBE SPAM

To be scrupulously fair about this, we do admire and respect these people's work rate. To manage to insert an advert for your hot MILF swingers site into the discussion thread under nearly every single video posted by the millions of YouTube users worldwide does represent a level of dedication and downright industriousness that we're always being told is lacking among the young people nowadays.

It's still grossly stupid and highly irritating, however. All you're trying to do is while away the seconds until death by watching obscure clips of The Faces whom, let's face it, you don't even like that much but it beats working . . .

don'tstopthenight (2 days ago):
The early 70's . . . Rod was true to his rock n roll roots back then, solo or with The Faces. Excellent!

bluemagoo (1 day ago):
Is this Rock 'n' Roll?????

xmo99er (1 day ago):
Looks like Nicky Hopkins on piano. These guys rocked, what a great band.

captaincaptain (1 day ago):
Nope . . . that's the great Ian McLagan . . .

cottoneyejoe (2 days ago):
Definitively Faces it was a great band.
Awesome

zebb27849 (2 days ago):
for hot teen babes, go to hotteenbabes.com. they're hot.

yeswe'realonenowtiffany2 (2 days ago):
Thats an Armstrong plexiglass guitar Woody is using. The prototype was used by Keith during the Stones' 69 tour.

A variation on this is certain users' obsession with grading any female by how "hot" she is. Any female at all. This is not limited to music videos featuring gyrating honeys, but extends to serious actresses involved in moments of high drama (say, Charlize Theron in *Monster* ("hot") and even footage of German Chancellor Angela Merkel . . .

hoochiecoochieman (6 days ago)
SOOOOOOOOO HOT.

jimbo12 (6 days ago)
She's, like, the hottest.

hoochiecoochieman (6 days ago)
Yeah, a hottie.

jimbo12 (6 days ago)
Hot stuff.

hoochiecoochieman (6 days ago)
A hot one. Hot--to--trot.

mangodave (2 days ago):
I don't like her.

yeswe'realonenowtiffany2 (2 days ago):
Thats a vintage Ralph Lauren blazer she's wearing, from the Spring-Summer 98 collection. The one with the three-button cuffs.

zebb27849 (2 days ago):
for hot teen babes, go to hotteenbabes.com. they're hot.

YUMMY MOMMIES

Don't just lie there! It's been two hours since you've given birth. Get on that treadmill now. Or you're never going to "snap right back" by the end of the frigging week. Society expects! Or, at least, a certain part of vile Hollywood monied tosspot society expects. Before your newborn's first month, you must be playing *Bartok for Babies* while baking organic muesli bars. If you do not spend on your child in its first three months the same as the average yearly wage, then your child will be ugly and stupid. And who wants that?

The country is now so crazed with the desire to produce "alpha children" that some toddlers are even going to Japanese classes. One recent article reported that one two-year-old had reportedly been taught Roman numerals, French, and Latin. At nursery, instead of mixing with other children, she just stood howling—possibly in disbelief at the quality of her peers' conjugation.

We wonder what's the Japanese for "teenage nervous breakdown."

Z

Z-LIST CELEBRITIES AS FUCKWIT PUNDITS

On what had to be the slowest news day of the year, ABC News's Julia Bain reported that Stephen Baldwin—aka the born-again Baldwin or the Baldwin who looks like a retarded Muppet—decided, after much "homework," that he is endorsing Senator Sam Brownback in the 2008 presidential race. Thank God! Now we know who to vote for!

Except that Brownback dropped out of the race a mere two months after Stephen's endorsement. Good call, Stevie. Oh, and also: I am not taking political advice from the second lead from *Bio-Dome*.

Harry Belafonte went and did one better, going to Venezuela and calling President Bush "the greatest terrorist in the world." Careful, Harry! Osama hates being snubbed. He's already got a long list of U.S. celebs willing to pass off his own big moment as the work of the famously competent U.S. government. Charlie Sheen saw what was happening. He was there. Well, he wasn't there, but he saw it on TV: "It just didn't look like any commercial jetliner I've flown on any time in my life and then when the buildings came down later on that day I said to my brother 'call me insane, but did it sorta look like those buildings came down in a controlled demolition?' "

Call him insane? No, call him some kind of special genius! The government must be so pissed. They'd gotten thousands of conspirators committed to secrecy on pain of death, covered all their tracks, and thought they'd gotten away with mass murder. They hadn't reckoned on Charlie Sheen, though.

Right at this moment, they're probably yelling at each other in some bunker in Nevada: "Damn that Charlie Sheen—looks like we really underestimated that guy! We should have remembered that he'd be seeing it all on TV. But how did he pick up all that knowledge about the physical properties of skyscrapers? We just thought he was an expert on group sex . . ."

Z-LIST CELEBRITIES SAVING THE PLANET

Saving the planet is one of the major challenges facing the planet. Luckily, the celebrities know the score and are fighting—literally fighting—to do their bit. It's almost—*almost*—enough to make you think.

The poster child of worthless celebrities, Paris Hilton, is now a green-flag-waving environmentalist. While in Berlin promoting a new sparkling wine sold in cans (no joke, and no, we don't know what that means, either), Paris proudly told an entertainment blog that she "turns off the lights, doesn't leave the TV on or the water running when she leaves her house." That's not environmentalism; that's just leaving your house. It's common fucking sense! Did you used to flood the house *every* time you went outside?

Cameron Diaz also attempted to encourage environmental awareness with her MTV ecotourism show *Trippin*. The series showed Diaz and her famous friends touring developing nations, often in a full-size Chevy SUV—despite several on-screen, anti-SUV factoids detailing how environmentally unfriendly SUVs are. More importantly, it gave Drew Barrymore the rare opportunity to brag on TV, "I took a poo in the woods hunched over like an animal. It was awesome."

Most moving of all is the contribution of John Mayer, the Live Earth performer who has used his position of power to tell people all about the problems facing the world and how we must all . . . do pretty much fuck-all! "Pick one thing to change this year, and keep the rest of your life the same," he ordered his followers on a 2007 blog.

None of that "brow-beating people" with all that negative shit. You've just gotta take it nice and easy: "I drive a Porsche SUV, I still drink lots of bottled water, and I will be flying private charter several times during my summer tour. However, my bus has been converted to Bio-Diesel . . ."

One step at a time, people! Converting the world economy to avoid global catastrophe is actually just a case of "trying to be healthier," like nibbling on the odd grape and doing sit-ups. Then we'll be sweet!

But surely, if you are dipping your toe into green waters to tell everyone about how they shouldn't get too worked up about things that are worth getting worked up about or you'll just end up turning people off and then no one will do anything, while the entire world burns around our melting ears, then what you essentially are doing is WASTING EVERYONE'S FUCKING TIME.

Acknowledgments

Steve Lowe and Alan McArthur woud like to thank everyone they have worked with at Little, Brown Book Group in London and Grand Central Publishing in New York.

Brendan Hay would like to thank: my lovely wife, Jennifer Chen, for being a rock star; my parents, John and Maureen Hay, for encouraging my writing; my managers at Tom Sawyer Entertainment, Rachel Miller and Jesse Hara, for keeping me busy, as well as their assistant Rachel Tobias for keeping them organized; Ben Greenberg and Bob Castillo at Grand Central Publishing for all their help and guidance; Ben Karlin for putting in the kind word that got me involved in this project; and my cat, Bentley, for keeping me company during my long hours at the computer.